BRIGHT NOTES

TOMORROW AND YESTERDAY AND OTHER WORKS BY HEINRICH BÖLL

Intelligent Education

Nashville, Tennessee

BRIGHT NOTES: Tomorrow and Yesterday and Other Works
www.BrightNotes.com

No part of this publication may be used or reproduced in any manner whatsoever without written permission, except in the case of brief quotations in critical articles and reviews. For permissions, contact Influence Publishers http://www.influencepublishers.com.

ISBN: 978-1-645424-32-1 (Paperback)
ISBN: 978-1-645424-33-8 (eBook)

Published in accordance with the U.S. Copyright Office Orphan Works and Mass Digitization report of the register of copyrights, June 2015.

Originally published by Monarch Press.
E.S. Friedrichsmeyer, 1974
2020 Edition published by Influence Publishers.

Interior design by Lapiz Digital Services. Cover Design by Thinkpen Designs.

Printed in the United States of America.

Library of Congress Cataloging-in-Publication Data forthcoming.
Names: Intelligent Education
Title: BRIGHT NOTES: Tomorrow and Yesterday and Other Works
Subject: STU004000 STUDY AIDS / Book Notes

CONTENTS

1) Introduction to Heinrich Böll — 1

2) Tomorrow and Yesterday Overview — 6

3) Commentary — 15

4) Character Analyses — 17

5) Billiards At Half-Past Nine Overview — 22

6) Commentary — 32

7) Character Analyses — 34

8) The Clown Overview — 38

9) Commentary — 48

10) Character Analyses — 49

11) Group Portrait With Lady Overview — 52

12) Commentary — 64

13)	Character Analyses	65
14)	"My Uncle Fred" (1951)	68
15)	"This is Tibten" (1953)	73
16)	"Action Will Be Taken" (1954)	77
17)	"Murke's Collected Silences" (1955)	81
18)	"The Thrower-Away" (1957)	87
19)	"The Death of Elsa Baskoleit" (1951)	90
20)	"The Balek Scales" (1952)	94
21)	"And There Was the Evening and the Morning" (1954)	97
22)	"Like A Bad Dream" (1956)	101
23)	Criticism	104
24)	Essay Questions and Answers	108
25)	Bibliography	113

INTRODUCTION TO HEINRICH BÖLL

BÖLL'S LIFE

Heinrich Böll was born in Cologne, Germany, on December 21, 1917. His father owned a carpentry shop, placing the Böll family in the lower middle-class. Böll has remained faithful to this milieu and its people in many of his works. The simple values and the virtues characteristic of Böll's **protagonists** are those traditionally, and idealistically, associated with the German lower middle-class. Geographically, too, he has retained his roots. He still lives in his native city, and the locale of most of his important works in Cologne or the Rhenish area close to it. Böll was born a Catholic and remains a believer. However, the Rhenish brand of Catholicism is relatively liberal and unrestrained, as Böll indicates in his works by his numerous irreverencies toward the Church. His entire family - he was the sixth child - was characterized by this free, yet tenacious Catholicism, which was coupled with a lack of nationalism also typical of the Rhineland. These factors to a large degree helped Böll develop a strong sense of antipathy for, and independence of, the Nazi movement.

Though Böll managed to sidestep the Hitler Youth, he could not escape the draft. After high school, a brief apprenticeship in the book trade, and university study in German literature, he was inducted in 1939. Böll was wounded four times, but he was anything but a model soldier. In all the years until 1945 he managed to remain a private. Returning from English and American POW camps to his wife, whom he had married in 1942 and with whom he has three sons, Böll took up work as a census taker, and as a worker in his brother's carpentry shop. He also began to write.

Böll's first publications were a few short stories, followed by his first breakthrough, the novel *The Train Was on Time*, which appeared in Germany in 1949. His reputation as a writer grew steadily and he emerged also as one of the most respected voices on political and social issues in Germany. Along with Gunter Grass, Böll was able to break the tradition in Germany according to which the literary writer is to remain aloof from politics. Böll became a personal friend of Willy Brandt and he urged his countrymen to vote for Brandt's party in order to effect a modicum of spiritual renewal that, in Böll's view, Adenauer's Christian Democrats had failed to generate after the war.

All of Böll's involvement, however, was critical. For all his immense success, he felt progressively alienated in Germany. For a number of years, he took frequent trips to Ireland, where he maintained a cottage, in order to find solace in a country more to his liking. With the election of Brandt, however, Böll found the political and social climate less impalatable. He now retreats to a cottage in the Eifel region near Cologne. Böll's political involvement has brought on several public assaults on him. Most notably his calling for a fair trial for the Baader-Meinhof group (leftist revolutionaries involved in robbery and manslaughter) netted him the wrath of the right-wing press in Germany. Böll has traveled widely and has been to the United States several times for lectures and interviews.

Having won numerous literary awards in Germany, among them the two most prestigious, the Buchner Prize and the Prize of Group 47, Böll received the Noble Prize for literature in 1972.

BÖLL'S WORKS

Böll began his literary career with a number of stories and novels about the war. The novel *Der Zug war punktlich*, 1949 (*The Train Was on Time*, 1956), made him famous both with the critics and the general reading-public. The book deals with a German soldier who returns to the front from furlough. On his journey he realizes that he is going to die. With inescapable artistic logic, Böll makes the soldier's premonitions come true, showing the senseless, yet crushing fatefulness of war. In 1950, a collection of short stories appeared under the title *Wanderer, kommst du nach Spa . . .* (*Traveller, if You Come to Spa*, 1956). Here Böll adds to his repertory the **themes** of the soldier returning from the war, the post-war experience in Germany, and the topic of the black market. In 1951, *Wo warst du, Adam* (*Adam, Where Art Thou*, 1955), confirmed Böll's growing reputation as a novelist of stature. This novel is an absolutely convincing indictment of the war and the refusal of the participants in it to take individual responsibility for it.

In 1954 follows *Haus ohne Huter*, (*Tomorrow and Yesterday*, 1957). Here Böll turns to the victims of the war, the women and children in a fatherless world. Their plight is not only to survive without their husbands and fathers, but to suffer under the male survivors of the war, who are largely alive because they were more rapacious than those who died, and who now are the leaders of society.

Between 1955 and 1958, Böll published several collections of short stories, some of which had appeared earlier in newspapers. Among them are "And There Was the Evening and the Morning," "The Death of Elsa Baskoleit," "This is Tibten," "Murke's Collected Silences," "The Thrower-Away," and "Action Will Be Taken," all anthologized in *18 Stories*, 1966. In these collections Böll establishes himself as Germany's foremost satirist and shortstory writer.

Böll's reputation now founded solidly as a superb writer of short prose, he attempted to counteract the charge by some critics that he lacked the breadth for the long **epic** by producing his first major novel, *Billard um halb zehn*, 1959 (*Billiards at Half-Past Nine*, 1961). Though a long novel, it approaches the structural density of the short story and provides the definite proof that Böll is indeed the major novelist that many critics had claimed him to be.

Disillusionment with the German post-war scene, a leitmotif in Böll's works, reaches a note of stridency and the intensity of an absolute indictment of his society in *Ansichten eines Clowns*, 1963 (*The Clown*, 1965). It is the best satiric novel produced in Germany since the war. The **protagonist** in *The Clown* is so aggressive that he drives himself right out of the confines of society, losing his forum for effective criticism.

In his next novel, *Ende einer Dienstfahrt*, 1966 (*The End of a Mission*, 1968), Böll retreats a few steps as a critic to provide his hero with possibility of an efficacious social protest. His hero protests although he is an integrated member of society. He burns an army jeep, implicitly as a protest against the senseless and wasteful principles of order to which the army adheres, and explicitly, as a happening, in order to stir up a controversy over his act. He finds response and sympathy among the public.

Gruppenbild mit Dame, 1971 (*Group Portrait with Lady*, 1973), is as ambitious a novel as *Billiards at Half-Past Nine* and *The Clown*, and an extremely hopeful book. The individual, so battered and endangered in the contemporary novel, scores some triumphs in this novel. However, it takes a Leni Pfeiffer, a human being so exceptional as to be almost mythical, to survive the antagonistic forces in her society that are brought to bear upon her. Moreover, her individualism, though it is rather passive, generates respect and even love by many of those who know her.

Böll has done some work in drama - with little success - and has written a number of good radio plays, a **genre** still very popular in Germany.

In an interview on the TV show Book Beat, in the wake of the appearance of *Group Portrait with Lady*, Böll has indicated that he now wishes to return to the short story, with which he professes to have a special affinity.

TOMORROW AND YESTERDAY

OVERVIEW

GENESIS, TRANSLATIONS, INFLUENCES

The novel *Haus ohne Huter* (*Tomorrow and Yesterday*, 1957) appeared in serialization and shortly thereafter as a book in 1954. It was an immediate success and has been republished and reprinted several times in Germany. The novel has been translated into some sixteen languages. A degree of interpretation and misinterpretation is evident from the titles in other languages. In one translation, by Mervyn Savill (London, 1957), it is *The Unguarded House*, literally correct, but unpoetic, and in the other it is *Tomorrow and Yesterday*, by an anonymous translator (New York, 1957), poetic but inappropriate. In French it is *Children of the Dead*, in Dutch *House Without Fathers*, in Spanish *House Without Love*.

In 1954, Böll translated Salinger's *Catcher in the Rye*. Its main theme, like that of *Tomorrow and Yesterday*, is adolescence.

THEMES AND MOTIFS: SYMBOLISM

The major **theme** of the novel is Adolescence. The opening and closing **episodes** in the book are devoted to Martin Bach and Heinrich Brielach, the central characters, who are on the threshold of adulthood. As the story opens, Martin is in bed, about to go to sleep. He is thinking of comics, of Donald Duck and Hopalong Cassidy, and he derives pleasure from doing so. As the book closes, he is again about to fall asleep, but thinking of comics now seems dumb to him. He knows "that something was over: he did not know what, but something was over." Instead of comics, he now muses over a quote from the Bible; "If Thou, Lord, should mark iniquities," and a sentence from the catechism, "To what purpose are we on earth."

The process of learning about the world is very different for the two boys. For Martin, it is primarily exposure to sexual knowledge and the question of sin. For Heinrich, who for years has been in charge of his family's budget and at the age of five had been a black marketeer, adolescence holds out some hope for security. At the end of the book, he has been helped through a crisis of shame by Albert who, it seems, will be a father figure to him.

Carnal Knowledge

Sexual knowledge is one of the motifs conjunctive with adolescence. Böll uses it in leitmotif fashion. The aura of mystery, secrecy and sin it often holds for the adolescent is conveyed by the frequently repeated, and unvaried reference to the two boys Martin comes across in the bushes: They "had done something indecent: scarlet faces, open flies and the bitter odor of cut greens." Furthermore, the taboo quality sex has for the uninitiated is brought out by Martin's and Heinrich's avoidance of vulgarisms for the sexual act. They refer to and think of it as "Vereinigung" (conjunction), a euphemism adults use, and the vulgar term for fornicating is simply "the word" for them.

The adolescence of Martin and Heinrich, both eleven-year-olds, is not a happy and normal affair. They experience it too young, and under extremely adverse conditions. Their fathers were killed in the war and as a result the boys lack guidance and security. Their world is not idyllic and their emotional state is generally one of anxiety. They live in a "house without guardians," to translate the title in yet another way.

Exposure

The notion of extreme vulnerability, indicated especially by Heinrich's fixed idea that he is walking over ice that is about to break, or by the slogan, dragged by the plane, "Are you prepared for the worst," has several corollaries. The strongest of these motifs is:

Lack Of Fathers And Husbands

To the boys, their fathers cannot even serve to give them a personal father-concept. Their pictures show them too young to be their fathers and the husbands of their mothers. Their mothers have never recovered from the loss of their husbands. Martin's mother, intelligent and stubborn, idolizes her dead husband to a point that he becomes simply irreplaceable. Heinrich's mother also remains loyal to her dead husband in a self-destructive way. She insists on making decisions that drive her lovers away. The effect the fatherless family has on the boys differs in the two cases. Heinrich has to be the backbone of his family, consisting of his mother, his baby sister and Leo, his mother's lover. He remembers several of his mother's lovers, designated as "uncles," the euphemistic parlance used in German in these situations. Heinrich, then, at the age of eleven, has to be the father in his family.

Martin is much more fortunate. His father's best friend Albert lives in the same house with him. Albert is the most positive male figure in the novel. He definitely has the quality to be a father. However, Martin's mother refuses to marry him. Although Albert helps Martin in his transition to adulthood, he lacks to Albert the primary requirement to be a full-fledged father. To both boys, a father is a father only if he is married to their mother. Albert's role as a father-figure is further weakened by the basic structure of the household in which they live. It is decidedly matriarchal. Martin's maternal grandmother dominates the family and frightens Martin much of the time.

Though there is order in the boy's lives - they go to school, they are exposed to the traditional rules of deportment - the moral structure of their world is hollow, not only for them, but for their mothers as well. Böll strongly delineates the concept of the family, and society at large, as threatened in post-war Germany.

Empty Order

The major cause for the lack of a meaningful order in Böll's post-war world seems to be the lack of fathers. Böll romanticizes his point somewhat, conveying the notion in this novel that the good by and large died in the war. Thus a world designed to be patriarchal is bereft of those who were equipped to provide moral leadership in it after the war.

Aside from the realization that fathers must be married to mothers, Heinrich's primary criterion for a father is a very external characteristic. Fathers to him are the only members of the family entitled to a breakfast egg. Food and eating play an important role in Böll's works. Eating to Böll is a communal act, it has a social bonding function. At Martin's house, eating is done separately. There is repeated reference to a sign in Martin's kitchen. On it is the German adage "Love goes by way of the stomach." Böll imbues this philistinism with meaning in the context of Martin's life. There are a number of tenants in his house, who in a sense form a family, but they all eat separately much of the time. They do not "break bread together."

Hope

The notions of exposure and anxiety are counterbalanced by the **theme** of hope, which is traceable throughout the novel. It is sounded indirectly already in the first chapter, and is several times repeated later in the story, by the Biblical verse "If Thou, Lord, shouldst mark iniquities, who shall stand." Upon its first appearance, Böll complements the line by a commentary from the catechism: "God in his love forgives any sinner who truly repents." In the context of Martin's life, whose faith is intact, and, incidentally, in Böll's work, religious hope is not an empty concept. The **theme** of hope running through the book proves efficacious in a concrete and secular perspective. At the end of the novel, both Martin and Heinrich are in Bietenhahn, a place of togetherness and peace. Albert has helped Heinrich through the worst moments of his life. Heinrich has found someone who understands him and who is fully compassionate with him. Uncle Leo has been replaced by the baker, a less objectionable figure. The Brielach's poverty will not be quite so dire. Albert's act of compassion has given Heinrich's mother new strength and has restored in her a measure of faith in men. Martin's mother, strange celibate that she is, is on the verge of becoming a woman again.

Absurdity Of The Soldier's Death

Though it seems that the mothers of Martin and Heinrich should have adjusted better to their husbands' deaths, Böll supports their refusal to forget by strongly underscoring the absurdity of a soldier's death. This is especially obvious in the case of Martin's father. He died as a result of refusing an officer the familiar du form of address, which the officer takes as an insult and as insubordination. The senselessness of his death is juxtaposed with another "senseless" death. Leen, Albert's wife, dies of a ruptured appendix. Though also very traumatic, this death does not paralyze Albert beyond a normal span of mourning. Although Leen's death could have been avoided, it is ultimately accidental, unlike the death of a soldier.

SYMBOLISM

In this novel, Böll strongly prefigures the central symbolism in *Billiards at Half-Past Nine*, the "sacrament of the buffalo," and the "sacrament of the lamb," which divide the world into carnivores, butchers and murderers on one hand, and their victims on the other. Martin's grandmother insists on turning him into a meat-eater. She does it with repulsively bloody meals in a restaurant. Martin hates meat; and all the customers around him, especially his grandmother, strike him as carnivores. What is more, Martin is obsessed with the thought that the meat that is eaten, and the bones that are sucked dry and cracked, are the flesh and bones of children. His father's murderer, Gaseler, indeed a member of the fraternity of the buffalo, has taken care of his war memories, as he says, by "slaughtering them away."

The Film

Tomorrow and Yesterday actually contains only one pervading symbol. To Martin, Heinrich and their mothers, their lives are strangely unreal. Böll uses the film as a symbol to indicate their alienated sense of reality. Martin's mother experiences some of the **episodes** in her life as a badly acted movie. Böll's symbol grows naturally out of the times in which he writes. During the grim post-war years the movies were an escape from an unbearable reality.

The Jam Buckets

A marginal, yet frequent symbol are the jam buckets which Martin's father and Albert encounter everywhere they go as soldiers. Since they had a hand in designing the label, and since the buckets are from the jam factory owned by Martin's grandfather, the buckets stand for personal involvement, guilt, and complicity in the war. Böll subtly and ironically connects in this symbol the chiliastic element inherent in the Nazi ambitions with the apocalyptic facts of the war. The labels on the buckets read: "He who still cans [his own] jam, is stupid." Explicitly, from the Nazi perspective this means that the glorious future about to be entered will render such labors as home-canning obsolete.

Implicitly, in the face of the **catastrophe** about to befall Germany, providing for the future is pointless.

STRUCTURE

The relationship of experienced versus remembered time is the main structural principle in the novel. The actual time is approximately one week in the summer of 1953. The remembered time goes back to around the turn of the century. There are some references to the childhood of Martin's grandmother. In flashbacks. Böll juxtaposes the remembered past with the present. Generally, in the adults, the memories are overpowering because they signify loss of content in their lives. Especially in Martin's mother they are difficult to expurgate because she insists on extending the past into the present and even into the future. She continues to imagine what her life would be now and in the future if her husband had not been killed. But the novel ends not on the note of memories, but of reality. And, as has been said already, reality contains some hope for the principal characters in the novel.

LITERARY POINT OF VIEW

The narrator of *Tomorrow and Yesterday* is omniscient. In fact, occasionally, his omniscience spills over on his characters. The most conspicuous example is the hotel scene when Martin's parents check out to make room for the sergeant and his wife. Apparently meeting this sergeant and his wife for the first time in her life, Nella knows who he is and even that he will die. Predominantly, the novel is a third-person narrative. There are some segments, however, in which Böll employs dialogue.

STYLE

Böll's style translates rather well in this novel. By and large, it gains a bit in terseness, but loses some of its **epic** flow and a certain aura of sadness the German suggests. Böll's **diction** is restrained. It avoids surprise effects. The language is rather colloquial. It is markedly free of intellectualisms, which is in keeping with the rather anti-intellectual stance Böll assumes in this novel. There are no vulgarisms in this book. Although Böll's language, especially in dialogue, is simple and colloquial, and though it deals with people like the foul-mouthed Leo, it never becomes naturalistic. Notwithstanding that Böll's work has been accused of exuding the stale odors of a petit-bourgeois kitchen, it is never vulgar. In some instances, his style is a symbolic **realism** of considerable power. In the restaurant scene, in which Martin is to be turned into a proper meat-eater, the processes of eating are very realistically shown, but the symbolic meaning of the **episode** as an attempt to initiate Martin into the congregation of the carnivores is equally clear. Occasionally, Böll rises to pure **realism**, a style in which the symbolic intent is totally unobtrusive. This is the case in the scene of Leen's death. There is tension, sweep, and absolute fidelity to the essentials of the event.

TOMORROW AND YESTERDAY

COMMENTARY

The strength of this relatively early work of Böll's is its sharp-eyed view of the German post-war scene. But artistically the novel is uneven. It lacks discipline in some instances. As has been mentioned already, Böll permits his characters to be omniscient in some cases, a breach against the **realism** of the book. Now and then Böll lapses into cliches, for example when the school children ask their teacher if "heaven is the black market where you can buy everything." Occasionally, Böll too obviously uses his characters as mouthpieces of his own feelings. Nella's attack on the pseudo-intellectuality of her friends is simply too excessive to be Nella's. Schurbigel, the most unlovable intellectual of the lot, carries Böll away into a technical inconsistency. Before the war, Schurbigel tried to persuade Nella's husband and Albert to enter the SA in order to be a Christian sourdough in this Nazi organization. This indicates that Schurbigel was a "Christian" already in those years. But elsewhere in the novel Böll says that Schurbigel "discovered the immense attractions of religion after the war."

But there is also much evidence of tremendous talent in this early work. One example: Albert at one point recognizes Nella's shortcomings fully. Exhausted and disheartened by his insights, he takes a bath. Lost in his depressing thoughts, he drops a cigarette butt into the tub, watching it dissolve and blacken the water. The image is a perfect corollary to Albert's state of mind. His hopes of marrying Nella are dissolving; his image of her is becoming more and more tainted.

A final criticism of *Tomorrow and Yesterday* concerns Böll's treatment of women. In his efforts to show the negative aspects of the matriarchal phase after the war, he overdraws his lines. The women are simply too inept to be true. Heinrich's mother is incapable of handling the household money while her eleven-year-old boy is. Martin's mother and grandmother are ridiculous in their attempts to have the roof fixed, while Albert manages to do so in no time at all. A more subtle indication of Böll's overdrawing his lines is the frequently repeated scene in which some woman, but never a man, shouts at her child "watch out," or "don't go near there," implying that women are equipped to watch out only for the physical safety of children, capable only of commands, not of guidance.

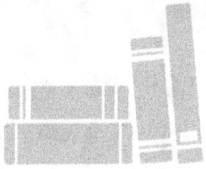

TOMORROW AND YESTERDAY

CHARACTER ANALYSES

MARTIN

Martin is a sensitive eleven-year-old boy with a religious conscience. He is fascinated with the elements of sex involved in his adolescence. But there are no signs of experimentation. He is interested in a moral understanding of the relationship of sex, lust, and love as he observes it, or the absence of it, in the adults around him.

HEINRICH

Heinrich. Much more worldly-wise than Martin, he is a boy faced not so much with moral questions but with problems of survival, both in the physical as well as in the psychological sense. He is obsessed with the feeling that he is walking over ice that is about to break any time.

ALBERT

Albert, in addition to Glum, is the only male in the book who has survived the war morally intact. He is the only person who could be an effective father. Albert loves Martin; and to become his father, he continues to ask Martin's mother to marry him.

GLUM

Glum miraculously survived being a human sacrifice in his primitive Siberian tribe, being wounded in the war, and a concentration camp. He is a sort of a noble savage who has grown so much intellectually that he reads and understands works on moral theology. Glum's function in the novel is primarily to offset Martin's grandmother, the matriarch. Though not a father, Glum is a representative of the Father World in the Jungian sense. This world is the intellectual and ordering principle. Glum, who paints a gigantic map of the world as he sees it, is an indication that Böll does not think that the patriarchal principle is dead, although its best representatives have been killed in the war. Significantly, Glum is not German. The moral leadership that the father world provides, Böll seems to indicate, must come from outside of Germany. There may even be a trace in the figure of Glum of the notion that Russia will provide that leadership. If so, Böll at the time of the novel seems to regard Socialism as a very positive force, for Glum is portrayed in a very favorable light. As it were, Böll would think of Russian Socialism as an ideology borne by noble primitives, full of survival power and innate goodness. The fact, however, that Glum does not return to Russia after the war seems to imply that Böll distinguishes between Socialism, its potentiality as a humanistic ideology on one hand, and Bolshevism on the other.

THE GRANDMOTHER

The Grandmother, like Glum, is best understood in Jungian terms. She is the matriarchal concept incarnate, a Great Mother figure.

She terrorizes the household with her frequent and frightening fertility and renewal rites, triumphantly going around the house shouting that there is blood in her urine. Though seemingly not ill, she insists on some kind of injection after blood shows up in her urine. The shot transforms her into a young-looking female. Faithful to the Great Mother archetype, she is both menacing and good. She likes to help people in need but she is also a savage who wants to transform Martin in her own image. Periodically, she subjects him to religious instruction that she perverts to conclude on a primitive note. She wants Martin to remember the name of his father's murderer so that revenge can be taken when he is found.

NELLA

Nella, Martin's mother, is in a sense like the grandmother. But the independence and autonomy of the rich old woman is in Nella the stubborn celibacy of a female paralyzed by the memory of her dead husband. Nella's "chastity" is somewhat perverse. She flirts, spends weekends with men now and then, but insists that she has not "really" slept with anyone since her husband died. She is a bit of a cynic who quite literally views her present life as scenes from a bad movie. She lacks honesty, for although she hates the intellectuals who are exploiting the poetry of her dead husband, she goes along with them. In the end of the novel, however, she breaks with them.

LEEN

Leen, Albert's dead wife, is Nella's positive complement. Böll's love for the Irish is visible in this idealized female. Unlike Nella, Leen is honest about her sexual appetites. She is wild and absolutely oblivious to orderliness. She wears a pressed dress only once, for her wedding, and looks bad in it because it is pressed. She hates shelves and storage cases, and she insists on keeping her belongings on a bed, to be swept off on the floor at night, and to be piled on again during the day. But Leen has an astute sense of inner order. She identifies sex and marriage. Although a hot-blooded female, she refuses premarital sex, while Nella, conversely, plays with sex. In her relationship with her dead husband, it was he who refused premarital sex.

HEINRICH'S MOTHER

Heinrich's Mother is a simple type who wishes to lead an ordered life but who is incapable of planning or working towards it. Thus she has a series of lovers, who, as they appear and disappear, contribute to Heinrich's sense of anxiety. But she is not without character. She once insisted on an abortion; once she insisted on keeping a child, in both cases knowing that her respective lover would leave her in consequence of her decision. She cares deeply for her children and at the end of the novel gives indication that her sense of autonomy is growing.

SCHURBIGEL

Schurbigel is a portrait of the opportunistic pseudo-intellectual. He is full of brilliant phrases and insights, but his intellect has no moral dimension. Böll hates this type. We will encounter it again in *The Clown* and in "Murke's Collected Silences."

GASELER

Gaseler is the murderer of Martin's father. He is petty, ambitious, competitive, amoral, intelligent; thus he is equipped to be highly successful. He must be understood as prototypical of those who engineered Germany's fantastic post-war recovery, which to Böll, largely lacked a moral dimension. Gaseler is one of those who survived the war, not so much by luck, but at the expense of others, of those belonging to the fraternity of the victims, like Martin's father.

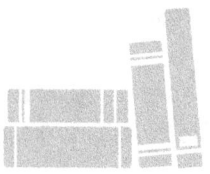

BILLIARDS AT HALF-PAST NINE

OVERVIEW

GENESIS, TRANSLATIONS

This novel, too, appeared first in serialization, in the *Frankfurter Allgemeine Zeitung*, and as a book in the same year, 1959. The German title is *Billard um halb zehn*. It was a tremendous hit, especially with the critics who found in its highly disciplined structure definite and conclusive proof of Böll's artistic depth and power. The novel was brought out subsequently by several publishing firms and in many reprintings in Germany.

There are at least eighteen translations of the novel. Only the French translation really changes the title, to The Two Sacraments, thereby emphasizing the moral content of the novel. The English translation, now available in paperback (McGraw-Hill) appeared in London in 1961.

THEMES AND MOTIFS

The central **theme** in *Billiards at Half-Past Nine* is Order. The theme is first of all exemplified in its negative manifestation by the Nazi era, the "new order," which sanctioned brutality and murder under the pretext of "law and order." The positive corollary to this perverted order is the object of the novel's quest. Schrella, returning to German in 1958, finds that there is "no political chance" for the country. He strongly intimates that Robert Fahmel in the political context has failed to become the shepherd of his fellow human beings he is equipped to be by virtue of his character. Robert Fahmel, in other words, is precisely the kind of man post-war Germany needed in the position of leadership. He has an impeccable political past; he is admired, honest and just. But Robert Fahmel is an intensely private man. The humanity evident in him, and in all those who have not eaten of the "sacrament of the buffalo," rests on private relationships. It is not the ideological, abstract humanitarianism characteristic of the politician. Robert Fahmel's notion of order has very little to do with our concept of democracy, or for that matter with any form of government or political system. It is Christian; it favors the exploited and oppressed, the perennial victims of those in power. Fahmel is therefore unsuited to politics, to the game of power. The novel in this sense is quite pessimistic. It points to the basic dichotomy between humanitarianism and politics. In another respect, however, *Billiards at Half-Past Nine* is a hopeful novel. It points to the hope inherent in the existence of that minority Böll calls the lambs, the human beings who will not eat of the "sacrament of the buffalo."

Robert Fahmel's affinity for order is a very personal one. It is symbolized by his highly formulated life, the playing of billiards, the regularity of his activities, his profession as architect, even his expertise as a demolitions expert. In the private dimension he becomes the shepherd he is meant to be. He adopts the hotel boy Hugo. In fact, his entire surviving family manifests the right priorities. They weigh the building as well as the destruction of the abbey St. Anton against the death of those they loved. In that light, the abbey, although it is the family's claim to fame, does not matter.

The Good Shepherd

Supportive motifs are used by Böll to further define the **theme** of order. The command "tend my sheep,' specifically applicable to Robert Fahmel, is also heeded, but in perverted form, by the sheep woman who poses as the founder of a new religion, in which only externals are important. She advocates sheep milk, while in private she hates it, and exudes the odor of sheep dung to heighten the impression of authenticity. She is in hot pursuit of Hugo whom she wishes to make the masthead of her religion. In addition to indicating that an external order must have an inner meaning, Böll, in making the sheep woman a **parody** of Christ, leaves no doubt that the sacrament of the lamb, as well as its opposite, the sacrament of the buffalo, must be linked to a Christian frame of reference.

Tyranny Of Externals

The superficiality of the society Böll depicts becomes especially manifest in the figure of the "ugly woman." No one except Hugo dares to look at her. But there is no indication of ugliness in this creature's personality. She is an outcast simply because of her appearance. In fact, she is characterized by a sense of justice and kindness. She will not subject those outside of the hotel to her grotesque appearance. They do not deserve it, she explains. The clientele of the Hotel Prince Henry, however, do. They are the rich and the powerful. They are those, by and large, whose values are mirrored in the external appearance of this woman through which alone they relate to her.

Life's Purpose

The exclamation "whatforwhatfor," repeated in leitmotif fashion, is first of all a complaint by the lambs who are lost, who are without a shepherd, who see no point in going on with life in the face of its blows. But in German the phrase "wozuwozu" also means "to what purpose" and thus it points to the Christian context, in which life does indeed have a purpose. The individual is to be held accountable, to retain "a pure heart," to reject the sacrament of the buffalo.

The Call To Resist

The quote from the poet Holderlin, "in compassion, the eternal heart remains firm,' is another leitmotif that provides definition to the moral perspective. To be a lamb does not mean that it is blessed to be butchered. The command, "shepherd my lambs," in this book refers to earthly well-being. Böll's theology is not escapist. Moreover, Robert Fahmel does not comfort Hugo with the prospect of heavenly justice, but he makes him his son. Schrella and Johanna Fahmel do not simply forgive and forget as Nettlinger wishes them to do. There is militancy in them. They are good as well as tough.

SYMBOLISM

The "sacrament of the buffalo" is partaken of by the powerful in this world, the exploiters, those with a will to subdue others. Specifically, it refers to Germany's militarist and nationalist establishment which led Germany and much of the world to ruin. Hindenburg, a mediocre German general of the First World War, whom the Germans stylized into a war hero and who because of his simplistic patriotism became the rallying point and father figure to the nationalists in the twenties, is specifically referred to in the context of the sacrament of the buffalo. The "sacrament of the lamb" clearly has a Christian frame of reference. It refers to those who will not exploit, who will not be the aggressors in human relationships, and who will rather die than kill. Specifically, the lambs are the innocent victims of the war and the Nazi atrocities.

It is interesting to note that, in the polarity of victim and victimizer, Böll uses the buffalo rather than the wolf to indicate the victimizer. By doing so, he avoids making the frame of reference entirely Christian. Rather, choosing the buffalo as the symbol for the victimizers, Böll stresses the notion of power as the greater determinant in the picture than evil. The buffaloes are not devils; they simply bulldoze their way to the top of the hierarchy that happens to be in power. By linking the victimizers to the buffalo Hinderburg, Böll indicts the German power structure that led to Hitler; his reference is a general one: It is to the politicians of a certain type, the Nettlingers of the world, the bad shepherds.

The Wild Boar And The Printing Presses

The symbolism of the lamb and the buffalo is complemented and somewhat more closely defined by the juxtaposition of the wild boar, forever displayed in front of Gretz's store, to the printing presses, forever producing literature of edification. It seems that the sacrament of the buffalo has an ally in the appetites of man. Man is a meat-eater. The restaurant scene in *Tomorrow and Yesterday* comes to mind. There, we recall, the grandmother is intent on stuffing Martin with half-cooked meat. The sacrament of the lamb, on the other hand, may gain support by the written word, if it is mindful of a moral perspective.

STRUCTURE

Thematic Structure

In *Billiards at Half-Past Nine*, Böll makes massive use of metaphors, symbols, and images that point to the main **theme** of order. Among them are the game of billiards with its constantly different variations and configurations of the balls, the profession of architecture with its components of dynamics and statics, and the baseball game in which Robert Fahmel hits the ball according to a precisely figured mathematical formula. Repeatedly, there are references to schematic movements, as for example the precise curve at which the old Fahmel moves his leg when walking, or the patterns in which the waiters at Cafe Kroner move, reminiscent of dance figures. Robert's hundred-meter-dash practice is built up according to exact progressions. Both Robert Fahmel's and his father's lives are conducted according to precise daily schedules.

Some of these examples of the human sense of order seem spurious. The breakfast of old man Fahmel contains a cheese concoction he never really liked; yet he continues to consume it until his eightieth birthday in order to keep his personal legend intact. Some examples of organization seem perverse, like the destruction of the abbey. Others are obviously meaningful. Among them the daily routine of billiards is the foremost. The playing is the backdrop to the highly personal and confessional conversations between Robert Fahmel and Hugo. Here Böll signals that all human endeavors are performed before a tapestry of meaning. Action is not random. It has purpose. Human endeavors in this novel are abstracted, concentrated, categorized, blueprinted, calculated, compressed into formula, into designs, delineated in curves, into coordinates to indicate, above all, that all human activity has a reference to meaning. But for Böll this significance inherent in the process of categorization and formulation is not a positive value per se, as might be the case for the scientist, for example. For Böll, as for every serious writer, meaning inherent in human activity must be given profile by the moral perspective. To Böll, order becomes essentially human only when it reflects a moral premise accepted or rejected by personal decision. For example, the social pretensions of old man Fahmel do not constitute an indictment. Although old man Fahmel may be a bit of a phony, he never in his life opted for the sacrament of the buffalo. In the framework of this novel the subjugation to the will of the stronger, the willingness to be used against one's moral convictions, constitutes the criterion for a meaning denied to human existence. Thus the building of the abbey, its cultural significance, become secondary in the light of the fact that some of its monks are infected by Nazism.

The symbols of the lamb and the buffalo, though they have religious connotations, must not be taken out of the context of the technical structure of the novel. Böll's book is more than a moralistic tract. Thus these symbols are not merely sacramental, but are foremost that element of calculation in the dynamic and static structure of the personality which determines if the person will stand or fall as a human being.

Time Structure

A second element of the novel's structure is purely technical. Böll makes use of highly sophisticated time schemes. The span of action is one day, September 6, 1958, the eightieth birthday of old man Fahmel. One by one, the leading characters are put on stage, and in interior monologue or in conversation the past is brought up to date. Although each character adds detail and his personality to the events remembered, the spectrum covered is essentially the same. In other words, a given character does not reminisce about people or events in which none of the other characters are interested. Thus, the focus gradually narrows down to the perspective of the two sacraments. The terms "sacrament of the buffalo" and "sacrament of the lamb" are used by the characters as if they were household words, indicating the central issues: What stand did people take during the Nazi years, and how do the members of the Fahmel clan relate their personal lives to these sacraments, having built the great abbey of St. Anton (Heinrich), destroyed it (Robert), and rebuilt it (Joseph)?

Acceleration

Near the evening of September 6, there is a noticeable acceleration in the flow of time. Its crescendo is the shot Johanna Fahmel takes at the anonymous minister of state, a gesture of equalization, of justice against the buffaloes of the world. At the birthday party following the shot there are further symbolic revelations of the values of the Fahmel clan. Old man Fahmel cancels his breakfast routine, living up to the recognition that it has been a phony ritual, and instead of smashing the cake model of St. Anton, as he felt the urge to do when it is brought in as a surprise by the Cafe Kroner people, he graciously cuts it up and serves it to his family. In view of the importance of communal eating in Böll's work, this act of eating the St. Anton cake indicates the proper relationships of the clan's life work to their moral character. In this moment of symbolic truth, the entire past of the Fahmel family, so intimately connected with the abbey, is integrated into the present, and this present is to the Fahmel clan an eternal moment, for it stands under the aegis of the sacrament of the lamb. Sacraments, as one of the Fahmels says, have the quality of being eternal.

The meeting of the temporal and the eternal is reached fully at the end of the novel, but Böll works toward it in many details throughout the novel. For example, he neutralizes the fundamental characteristic of time, its chronological flow, by switching time segments. Remembering his anticipation of the finished abbey, old man Fahmel says, "I closed my eyes, felt the cold, which I would be able to feel only fifty years later." The present, the moment of remembrance, is connected with the past, but that past is projected into the future and experienced in terms that only the future can provide. Since the present moment of remembrance provides the entire perspective, the present moment is in control, thereby subsuming past and future, making the present a "temporal eternity," so to speak.

LITERARY POINT OF VIEW

Although there is much direct speech in *Billiards at Half-Past Nine*, the point of view is predominantly that of the narrator. He does not assume omniscience for himself, but relies heavily upon the information furnished by his characters. Unlike the traditional realistic storyteller who adheres to chronology and is faithful to detail as propellants of his plot, the narrator in this novel rather strikes us as the literary craftsman who skillfully manipulates his characters and the events to make his symbolic aims transparent. The result is that the characters sound and think very much alike. Several, for example, operate with the symbols of the sacraments of the lamb and of the buffalo as if they were real concepts as Nazism or Communism.

STYLE

The style of this novel seems more difficult than it actually is because of the complex time schemes. Once the reader begins to watch out for the dividing lines between discourse and interior monologue, between the present, the past and its various segments, he can make his way easily through the book.

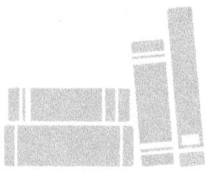

BILLIARDS AT HALF-PAST NINE

COMMENTARY

Billiards at Half-Past Nine is a much more consciously crafted novel than *Tomorrow and Yesterday*. In this later work, Böll's sense of storytelling is suppressed by the overriding rigorousness of the technical structure. But what Böll gains, especially in the eyes of those critics who understood *Billiards at Half-Past Nine* largely as the definite proof of Böll's artistic intelligence, he loses elsewhere. The characters are not as plausible as those in *Tomorrow and Yesterday*, notwithstanding the slanted view of women in that novel. It is only after we stop to tell ourselves that the technical architecture of *Billiards at Half-Past Nine* is the prerequisite medium for the message of the novel that we can tolerate the constant mouthing of symbols by the characters, as if the sacrament of the buffalo, for example, were a household word, and not a private symbol of Böll's.

Furthermore, the plot of this novel is somewhat insignificant. Events are so stylized by memory that their **realism** is rather thin. For all its flaws, *Tomorrow and Yesterday* shows more sweep, it mirrors more life, though it admittedly reflects less artistry than *Billiards at Half-Past Nine*.

Because of its hyperdeveloped artistry and its concomitant lack of **realism**, it is difficult to take the book very seriously as a piece of social criticism. The situation in the West Germany of 1958 does not emerge clearly before the reader; the characters are largely bloodless, and they lack their own voices and, even more critically stated, their own identity. When we are told that Robert Fahmel is a great runner at the 100-meter-dash, we do not feel that this truly characterizes him. It means, rather, that Böll is incorporating yet another design feature when he has Robert build up his practice races by a precision formula, and, significantly, not against some person, but against the clock. If we concur that Böll in *Billiards at Half-Past Nine* submitted his masterpiece, as many critics feel, he has done so only in the sense of expert craftsmanship, not in the sense of **epic** power and sweep.

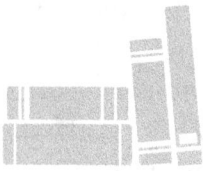

BILLIARDS AT HALF-PAST NINE

CHARACTER ANALYSES

ROBERT FAHMEL

Robert Fahmel is the central character of the novel. He belongs to the middle generation of the Fahmels. He has blown up the abbey his father built and which his son helps to rebuild. Robert is the Fahmel most exposed to accepting responsibility in the clan. He has committed himself openly against the sacrament of the buffalo, stands beside Schrella, and becomes a father to Hugo. He furthermore is unbending in his open rejection of the buffaloes even in post-war Germany, where they mask as committed democrats. His central position in the cast of characters is also indicated by his daily routine of billiards, the central **metaphor** for the quest of order. Robert Fahmel approaches the dimension of the heroic more closely than any other figure in the book.

HEINRICH FAHMEL

Heinrich Fahmel, Robert's father, is perhaps more easily appreciated by the reader than his son Robert. He is more willing to compromise than Robert and seems less aloof and cold. He seems to care more about being liked than does Robert. The reason lies in the fact that Heinrich is somewhat of an upstart. To make it in the world, he built a legend of style, regularity and trustworthiness around himself. He married the "right" girl, became wealthy and influential. But he does not lose his soul in the process, as many of Böll's wealthy figures do.

JOHANNA FAHMEL

Johanna Fahmel, his wife, is to a degree responsible for his integrity. She is an absolutist who has never made concessions to the buffaloes. She has called the Kaiser the "imperial fool," and has escaped death at the hands of the Nazis only because her family had her declared insane. Her sense of justice is so rigorous that, for example, she refuses to make use of extra food available to her family during the war. The Holderlin phrase "In compassion, the eternal heart remains firm" applies to her as much as it does to her son Robert.

SCHRELLA

Schrella, Robert's friend and eventual brother-in-law, is the lamb Robert protects during the ball game. Schrella is the perennial victim. Having fled Germany because of the Nazis, he is incarcerated upon his return because his name is still on the wanted persons list. Schrella indicts post-war Germany as a country unfit to live in. In his contact with his former tormentor Nettlinger, who has become commissioner of police after the war, Schrella's eternal status as a lamb becomes obvious. Nettlinger practically orders Schrella to take certain dishes, and Schrella goes along, but only to a point. He stops Nettlinger when his dignity is in danger of impairment.

NETTLINGER

Nettlinger is the chief buffalo in the novel. He is the type who will always be with the winning side and will always have his hands on the levers of power. During the war, he was a good Nazi, after the war he is a model democrat. Böll makes this prototypical politician and leader of men very believable mainly by granting him an element of good-naturedness. This, however, is not to be confused with a redeeming feature. Nettlinger's springing Robert from jail is at best arbitrary, at worst an act premised on the calculation that the Fahmel's social importance might be of help to him someday.

JOSEPH FAHMEL

Joseph Fahmel, Robert's son, is involved in rebuilding the abbey. He learns that his father has destroyed it and he is deeply troubled over it. His continued association with the project becomes questionable because he understands his father's reasons and because he learns that his grandfather always felt that the abbey was less important than the lives of the lambs that old man Fahmel loved.

EDITH

Edith, Schrella's sister, is among these lambs. Both Heinrich and Johanna Fahmel loved her deeply. In their memories, she is totally good, a saint.

HUGO

Hugo radiates the same blessedness of innocence that characterizes Edith. He, too, is a "lamb of god." His goodness would almost be troublesome to the reader as overdone, were it not clear that Böll concentrates on goodness in terms of participation in the sacrament of the lamb. Hugo thus is a martyr who always takes his sacrament, for he has been harassed and victimized all his life.

JOCHEN, THE HOTEL CLERK

Jochen, the Hotel Clerk, is a figure through which Böll assures us that he tolerates gradation of goodness. The only unpardonable sin is the partaking of the sacrament of the buffalo. Jochen, who knows that he is bribable, "corrupt to the marrow of his bones," is nonetheless a positive character, for he resists Nettlinger, and would do so with his life.

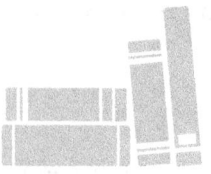

THE CLOWN

OVERVIEW

GENESIS, TRANSLATIONS

The Clown, 1965, appeared first in serialization in the *Suddeutsche Zeitung* in 1963, then in book form in the same year, under the title *Ansichten eines Clowns* (*Views - or opinions - of a clown*). Needless to say, its massive broadsides against the Catholic Church made it highly controversial from the start, especially in the light of Böll's well-known professions that he is a believing Catholic.

There are some twenty translations of the book. Practically every Socialist country has its edition. It is interesting to note however, that Böll is censored in the Socialist world. The East German edition deletes Schnier's sojourn to the German Democratic Republic, during which Schnier criticizes the regime. Most of the title translations retain the reference to "Ansichten," i.e., views, opinions. The exception is the English translation, and notably the French, *La Grimace*. The quality of the English translation by Leila Vennewitz is high. It is available in paperback.

THEMES AND MOTIFS

Empty Essence

It is obvious that *The Clown* is a highly satirical novel. The attack is directed at the Catholic Church. Schnier admits to only a handful of genuine Catholics in the world, the rest are the Sommerwilds and Kinkels, the "official," "modern," and "influential" Catholics. The basic weakness of their Catholicism is revealed by their criticism of Schnier. They accuse him of a lack of appreciation of an "abstract principle of order." To them, Schnier is devoid of a sense of the **metaphysical**. But Schnier's alleged deficiency is in fact an indictment of their brand of religiosity. They, and the Church with them, are given to an abstract Christianity.

Marriage

Marriage, for example, to the official Catholics, is no longer first and foremost a sacrament, as Schnier sees it, but a contract officiated over by church and state. These Catholics are interested in a "new order," to cite the title of a treatise by Kinkel, not as a new life, but as a new way to talk about life. The "new order" with which they toy does not mean anything to them existentially. Thus Kinkel's family life is full of antagonism and vulgarity.

Love And Sex

Schnier recognizes that the essences of Catholicism are empty, that they have no efficacy in the lives of the "believers." He counters their lives with his own, free of Catholic essences, but meaningful in the existential perspective. His "marriage" to Marie is not contractually validated, but based on a need that is both carnal and spiritual. In fact, the two cannot be split at all in Schnier. He reveals his love for Marie in a very unorthodox fashion. He goes to her and makes love to her. There is no courtship. Marie, although or because she is an innocent girl, recognizes this total lack of duality in Schnier and consents to sex, and by it, to love. Schnier's love for Marie, then, is both physical and spiritual, as Böll clearly indicates.

Monogamy

Upon losing Marie, Schnier is incapable of desiring another woman. In contrast to the "Catholics" around him who proclaim monogamy to be a virtue but believe that man is inescapably polygamous, Schnier is, in fact, "incurably monogamous." He has become one with Marie in the flesh and in the spirit and is destroyed by her rejection of him. The rejection is in large measure Schnier's own doing. His strength lies in the fact that his spirituality is totally intermeshed with his physicality and sensuality. But this is also his point of vulnerability. Although the spiritual is in him and in his life, he denies it. He is a disbeliever. When he is willing to marry Marie and even have their children raised Catholic, he fills Marie with a "**metaphysical** horror," because she senses not that he is capitulating, but that he is completely immune to the essences of Catholicism.

Schnier's Professionalism

Schnier states repeatedly that art means nothing to him. He dislikes discussions of art. He prefers to see himself as a craftsman. Again, his disregard for abstractions is involved. To him, art is not a concept, but something that is done. His attitude to art can be likened to his attitude toward religion. He is fond of singing liturgical music, that is, he loves ritual, religious action; he is immune to theology.

Art And Religion

Schnier's aversion for metaphysics and essences is ultimately rooted in his-state as a disbeliever and connected with his existential horror of nothingness. He is frightened to go on stage. Generally, he has to be pushed on it. Once there, he undergoes a process of being emptied out, he becomes a "marionette" by means of a "terrible coldness." In this state he is most effective as a clown and mime. To him this state is similar to the state of deep contemplation monks achieve. It is highly significant that Schnier defines this state by some of the words he found in mystical literature, such as "nothingness" and "emptiness." Of course Schnier interprets the union mystica in his fashion, confusing the taste of ultimate preparedness and receptivity, the emptiness to receive God, with the state of union with him. Or, to put it differently, when the mystics were full of God, they were empty of themselves. The process of artistic concentration, then is one of leaving himself, his existential mode, to become an essential type: The mime who is portraying not just a specific person, like a specific German general for instance, but the essential military type. In his art, then, Schnier must submit to a dimension he so arduously rejects in theory. The return to himself Schnier describes as "terrible"; it is an instant when the "string of the marionette breaks."

Schnier's Achilles' Heel

This moment of transcendence is more closely defined through Schnier's sister Henriette who would suddenly go vacant and drop everything she had in her hands. When asked what she thought of in these moments, she would reply "nothing." She would also refer to them as "eternities." The similarity to Schnier's state during a performance is clear. There is a state of transcendence, of touching essence. When Schnier speaks of the marionette, it is no mere **metaphor**. There are references in the novel to Heinrich von Kleist, a German dramatist for whom the marionette is a symbol of man. He describes it in terms of "essential action." To Kleist an individual who has lost his childhood grace can regain his equilibrium of action by an alignment with an essence above him. He no longer has the inner grace of the child, but is moved by an outside force that gives coordination to his actions and restores his grace. When Schnier refers to the horrible moment when the string of the marionette breaks, he implicitly reveals that there is some force that moves the string. But in his description of the moments of being a marionette as empty, Schnier indicates that he does not know or acknowledge the force pulling the string. Although he sees evidence of the transcendental in his life, and even though he has some affinity for essences, for he is a clown by choice, he denies them. Of course we can easily understand his posture as a disbeliever since the essences he negates are bankrupted by the Church and the believers like Kinkel and Sommerwild. Nonetheless, Schnier makes a mistake when he seems to identify the disreputability of the believers with proof against the existence of God. His own life and art prove the efficacy of God in him. Ironically, as Schnier denies God, he is His vehicle. In this he is the modern type of whom Rilke says:" "When God is in your heart / And reveals nothing at all / Then he is at work in it."

Schnier's concept of love and marriage, his reaction to Henriette's death, his conduct vis a vis the Nazis, his unerring sensitivity to evil prove that a moral force is at work in him. Though Schnier denies God and the Catholic faith, he admits to one essence. It is Marie. Without her, he can barely function at all. There is in him an element of enslavement to her, especially in terms of sex. Schnier's preoccupation with the act of sex with Marie is so intense that it is difficult not to think of Marie as a surrogate essence. Schnier, it seems, is in the position of Tannhauser who in his service to Venus is imprisoned in the Venus Mountain, the mons veneris, jeopardizing his soul.

Schnier As An Existentialist Type

To the theologian Paul Tillich the search for essences is for a God above the God who has in our world become an empty and sterile concept. Schnier denies essence because it is to him identifiable with an invalidated God. God is but a meaningless concept Kinkel and Sommerwild use in a juggling act for their own gratification. But God nonetheless seems to be in Schnier's heart, because he is, in Rilke's and Tillich's sense, not a believer in the traditional mold. Even Sommerwild recognizes some of this when he calls Schnier an "almost pure human being." Schnier thus can be called an existentialist type in the perspective of Christian Existentialism.

Schnier As A Social Critic

Schnier is a social critic both as a mime and in his personal relationships with others. In view of his profession, one may say that Schnier is a critic by type. By the intensity of his aggressiveness he reveals the scope of his type: He is the traditional challenger of literary **satire** whose critical thrusts aim at the very foundations of a given system. As Schnier challenges Catholicism, one of the very foundations of our world, he is caught in the no-man's land in which one set of beliefs has lost its meaning, but no viable new values have emerged as yet. Schnier's acerbity as the satiric challenger is explained by this impasse. He does not exhibit the serenity of the messiah who has a blue print for a new world in his pocket, nor does he make any of the conciliatory gestures that Böll's conservative satiric **protagonists** reveal in the satiric short stories. Schnier's quandary is that he hates "messy rooms, but is unable to straighten out things."

Though Schnier's life shows no codified revelation of a new spiritual order, it is a potential force in the right direction.

Epiphanic Moment

The spirituality that permeates Schnier's life is revealed above all in the epiphanic moment. Schnier says that he is a clown and that he "collects moments." We have already mentioned the curious "empty" moments in his and his sister's lives. But the moment reveals not only the spiritual, but also very glaringly the absence of it. Böll uses the damning phrase or the pregnant gesture to indicate this. As his mother rejects her son, she says, "I feel compelled to cast you out." His father places his hand on Schnier's shoulder, seemingly the only gesture of compassion he ever showed his son. The epiphanic moment may be signaled by spontaneous action as when Schnier takes the taxi, wanting to be with Marie and not caring if he alienated a friend.

SYMBOLISM

The Game Of Sorry

The game is a symbol of Schnier's art. Playing the game, he feels that "magnificent emptiness" Henriette experienced during her mystical moments. But these instances of nothingness also lasted an "eternity," and they "intoxicated" her. Schnier, then, is at once emptied and in contact with an essential from of being during the game. The game's purpose is to bring one's figures home. In the process, however, one must knock out the figures of the other players if one happens to land on the same field. Schnier as a critic has a purpose. He must prevail by knocking off his targets. But he does so by higher direction, if you will. He does not control the dice. He has become the marionette; he is in the state where some outside force controls the string. As a critic, his sense of criticism is automatic, operative whenever he encounters and senses deviation from his standard of human decency. The German name of the game is "Don't be Angry." It defines Schnier's role as the satirist who never attacks the people per se, only their foibles. Schnier admits to "love mankind, of which he is a member." In fact, the victims of his castigations are rarely mad at him for long. They like him despite the fact that he "knocks them off."

The Wounded Knee

The Wounded Knee indicates that any injury to Schnier, even if it is so clearly psychic as his loss of Marie, has a physical dimension. The knee, in fact, hurts as much as his soul. The tendency to translate abstractions and intangibles into the physical is evident throughout the book. When there is a reference to his grieving soul, Schnier insists on the word heart. When someone tells him his soul is lost, Schnier demands it back, saying that his soul is Marie.

Ability To Smell Over The Phone

This surrealistic element indicates Schnier's immense perspicacity regarding human beings. People are wide-open books to him. But his critical sense is moral not by reference to a spelled-out code of ethics; it is a sense, it is sensual. Schnier somehow can hear, see, even smell when something is wrong.

STRUCTURE

Time schemes are the prominent tectonic features of this novel. The outer time frame is extremely narrow. When Schnier arrives in Bonn, it is already dark. The month is March. When he returns to the station, it is half-past nine. Thus the time spanned is about three hours. The inner time frame is large. It reaches into Schnier's boyhood, and also into the future when Schnier images Marie's life to come. The intense compression of the inner frame is in fact a most fitting corollary to the thematic aspects discussed previously. Schnier collects moments pregnant with meaning. As these moments reveal an aspect of eternity, so past and future are embedded in the critical short hours after Schnier's return to Bonn.

In addition to time structure, which we found to be important also in the previously discussed novels, the structure of *The Clown* is also reflective of **satire** as we shall discuss it in the analysis of Böll's satiric short fiction later. We have characterized Schnier as the legitimate challenger of the system and have pointed to the reasons for his failure. The Biblical quote prefacing the novel alludes to both Schnier's role as pointing to a world of meaningful essences and to his incapability to make something explicit that has not yet come into being.

LITERARY POINT OF VIEW

The Clown is an intensely subjective book. The whole world is in the eye of the beholder, and it is Schnier's highly critical eye.

Since, however, Schnier's subjectivity in the satiric perspective has unquestionable objective validity, Schnier's subjectivism is at once objective. The best mode in which to deal with such a story is clearly the first-person narrative that Böll employs.

STYLE

Since *The Clown* is such a subjective account, highly charged with passion, the novel has a dramatic sweep that is superior to that of the two previously discussed novels. There are in *The Clown* few of the retarding structural markers that we found in *Billiards at Half-Past Nine*, like the repeated references to the dead boar hanging in front of the store, or to old man Fahmel's cheese breakfast.

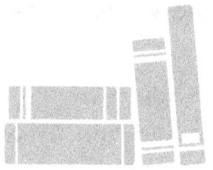

THE CLOWN

COMMENTARY

....

Although *The Clown* is an abrasive and irksome book, it may be Böll's best to date. There is really no sentimentality in it. Whereas in *Billiards at Half-Past Nine* most of the characters sounded like mouthpieces of the narrator, whose primary concern seemed to be to press them into service in the construction of the symbolic architecture of the book, in *The Clown* everyone speaks with his own voice, notwithstanding the fact that we hear everyone mainly through Schnier. Hans Schnier as a truly unique person is more believable when he claims to be able to smell over the phone than the Fahmels when they talk about the "sacrament of the buffalo."

Böll again attains the **epic** urgency we found in *Tomorrow and Yesterday*. But where in the earlier work we had to fault Böll for slanting the portrayal of women to fit his structural concerns, we can hardly fault him for the excessive broadsides against Catholicism in *The Clown*. It is not Böll, but Schnier who might be unfair. And if he is unfair, it is understandable. Schnier's reasons are not artistic, as Böll's are in *Tomorrow and Yesterday*; they are human and passionate.

THE CLOWN

CHARACTER ANALYSES

....

HANS SCHNIER

Hans Schnier has already been discussed as the satiric challenger and thus his self-centeredness is explainable as necessary to his aggressive form of being. His self-pity is primarily concerned with his physical state, and this must be so since his spiritual agony is experienced also as physical. Schnier's aggressiveness must be seen in similar fashion. He sees evil in the small concrete nuances of human behavior, in the daily trivia, where, of course, evil does flourish. Schnier sees the banality of evil, to use Hannah Arendt's phrase. By ordinary yardsticks Schnier is immensely obnoxious, though he may actually be much less aggressive than he portrays himself during these hours of crisis. Schnier is in the process of breaking away from society altogether. The satirist-clown must stand in it with one foot, and outside with the other to remain effective. Through the loss of Marie, Schnier loses his surrogate - his essence and strength and he becomes the pitiful outsider who is totally thrown back upon himself, the extreme existential loner. His conduct over the phone cuts all his life lines with society and he reaches the state of "freedom" that he momentarily anticipated when he had flopped on the stage and found himself without his oppressive headaches for the first time.

MARIE

Marie is an admirable woman and we cannot fault her for leaving Schnier. It is difficult to imagine a more understanding "wife." But Marie is a believing Catholic. Schnier himself grants her the status of authentic Catholicism. Therefore the essences that are empty to Schnier are not so to her. Her "**metaphysical horror**" sounds like a pompous phrase from Sommerwild or Kinkel, but it describes her attitude toward Schnier nonetheless. Schnier's professed lack of a **metaphysical** dimension must be frightening to her especially since she does not recognize that Schnier's moments of emptiness are in fact transcendental. When the two play "Sorry," she thinks of it as relaxation, and nothing else.

SOMMERWILD AND KINKEL

Sommerwild and Kinkel are captives of the empty doctrines of the Church. They are in love with Catholicism as a means to power and influence. Sommerwild is the more acceptable of the two. He recognizes that Schnier is an "almost pure human being," and he admits thereby implicitly that Schnier's aggressiveness is justified. But he, as the other Catholics in the circle, is unable or unwilling to shed the ballast of traditional religiosity and penetrate to that burdensome existential dimension of human purity and vulnerability Schnier inhabits.

SCHNIER'S MOTHER

Schnier's Mother is always in full sympathy with the forces in power, be they the Nazis or the Christian Democrats. She cheerfully sent Henriette to her death to defend the "holy German soil against the Jewish Yankees." After the war she becomes president of an organization working for the obliteration of racial problems. She feels compelled to "cast out" her son, the clown. She is unthinking, though she has intellectual and cultural pretentions. She moreover is extremely stingy, so much so that she kept her children on a starvation diet. Although she has no heart and understands nothing except the powers that be, she claims for herself that she is the only one in her family who understands people. Schnier's mother is one of Böll's matriarchs, strong, but ruthless in this case.

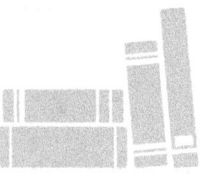

GROUP PORTRAIT WITH LADY

OVERVIEW

GENESIS, TRANSLATIONS

Böll has indicated that the incubation of *Gruppenbild mit Dame*, 1971 (*Group Portrait with Lady*, 1973) was a matter of several years; the writing, however, did not take long. As was the case with his previous novels, *Group Portrait with Lady* was an instant success in Germany, holding the top spot on the bestseller list for several months. It was singled out in the laudatio accompanying the Nobel Prize. However, it almost goes without saying that Böll would certainly not have received the award on the strength of this novel alone.

The translation into English by Leila Vennewitz is difficult to fault on technical grounds. But as is usually the case with translations, the negative aspects of an author's style tend to be magnified. At times, reading the English version becomes extremely tedious, especially during the first 150 pages. The reader who goes beyond this point in the book is likely to find it increasingly rewarding.

THEMES AND MOTIFS

One way of approaching *Group Portrait with Lady* is by way of comparison with *The Clown*. Both novels are largely definable in terms of their central character. One of Schnier's fundamental characteristics is his lack of affinity with, and lack of appreciation of abstract principles. The dimension of the **metaphysical** entered his life in rare moments, such as during a performance, and its meaning went largely unrecognized. They were more than anything else instances of empty transcendence. Thus, to Schnier, the spiritual is equal to valueless abstraction. Leni Pfeiffer, the heroine of *Group Portrait with Lady*, shares with Schnier the lack of appreciation of abstractions. But whereas the disbeliever Schnier is militantly against them, since they define the "spiritual life" of the society with which he is at odds, Leni has no such critical prejudices. Whereas Schnier is the aggressive and insecure existentialist, who rejects all essences as illusory, Leni's life never loses its inner balance. It verges on pure being. To her, the spiritual enters this world in a natural, not a miraculous form. Her life is not led according to rules or empty abstractions from social processes and hierarchical patterns which the establishment in *The Clown* passed off as being "Catholic" and "spiritual." Whereas Schnier is bankrupt when he is left by Marie, who is to him his spiritual dimension, Leni never leaves that condition which might be called the state of grace. The "Au" informs us early in the novel that Leni is well-nigh perfect. Her perfection shows mainly in the absence of dualities in her life. This makes it difficult to describe her. It must be done in terms of contradictions not existing in her, or by paradoxes Leni's life avoids.

Quest For Leni Pfeiffer

The quest for Leni Pfeiffer, the main **theme** of the novel, must proceed in terms of contradiction and paradoxes, but the object of the search is Leni as a human being of wholeness and integrity. It is the search for a model to those close to her.

Sensual Spirituality

Leni's sensuality is described as mystical to indicate the oneness of the opposites. The foremost example is her **climax** in the heather. She so opens herself to nature in its full bloom in this **episode** that she experiences a "fulfillment" just lying on the ground and looking into the sky. This element of being one with nature never leaves her in the sexual realm. She rejects beds, preferring the outdoors whenever possible. Leni dislikes the manifestations of life's dualities. Whenever there are abstractions involved in human processes, she is at odds with them. She is out of sympathy with religious instruction as too abstract, she fervently looks forward to partaking of the eucharist, to her the "bread of life," and is terribly disappointed to receive a paper-like wafer. She is a slow learner in school because the material taught has no sensual dimension, and she has trouble with music, though she is very musical, because she is incapable of grasping it through theory, and she even dislikes fancy cooking because of the "abstract" utensils she needs for it.

The Natural Miracle

There are no miracles for Leni. There are only "naturals," so to speak. She is visited by the Virgin Mary on her TV screen and finds it entirely in order. It never occurs to her to debunk the phenomenon by recognizing it as a reflection of her own face.

Natural "Unnaturalness"

As for Leni the supernatural is not "higher," or miraculous; the "subnatural" is not a matter of disgust for her. In fact, she is immensely curious about scatological phenomena because they are taboo in society. The "higher" and the "lower" dimensions are, if you will, all part of the fullness of life, and Leni means to include both. Her view is likened to that of the artist to whom every manifestation of existence is a true color on his palette. Once, when reaching into a clogged toilet bowl to unplug it, Leni declares that "our poets did not shy away from cleaning out a john."

Spiritual Sexuality

Leni's sexuality, though it is very powerful, is on all but one occasion a sensitive guide to a meaningful relationship with the man involved. Her only mistake is her husband Pfeiffer whose expertise on the dance floor fooled her into taking him for a worthwhile person. But his lovemaking is a true indication of his character. She is immediately repelled by it. All her other relationships have a spiritual dimension. With Erhard and Boris, the heather, with its mystical significance, is the bridal bed; with the Turk, compassion is in the foreground. Böll goes to incredible lengths to make the point that Leni's existence is not dichotomous. Although she has an alliance with Mahmet, Leni holds hands with, and kisses some of the men who desire her, indicating that her compassion for them is not merely abstract.

Leni As A Social Creature

Those who do not know Leni will vilify her. She is called a whore on the street; there are suggestions that she be "eliminated," even "gassed." Those who do not recognize her "pure form of being" see only sexuality in her sensuality. Since there are no categories at hand to judge Leni by, the general public applies the lowest denominator imaginable. There can be no doubt that Leni is a misfit. She is, for example, totally oblivious to the notion of profit and exploitation. For this reason she faces eviction by the Hoysers. However, she is "materialistic." She loves some pieces of her furniture so dearly that she "would walk the streets" to prevent losing them. Again, of course, Leni's lack of duality is visible here. She does not see an object in terms of its abstract monetary value, but in terms of its emotional meaning to her.

Leni, The Proletarian

Leni is called a proletarian. It is an equivocal term, indicating her status in her society as extremely low, but it also points to the potential social significance of her type. There is repeated reference to the "Soviet (i.e., proletarian) paradise in the catacombs," where Leni and Boris make love, and where their son Lev is born. There are also **allusions** made by the "Au's" informants that Leni, Boris, and Lev are the Holy Family. Leni especially, but also Boris and Lev, share characteristics that would qualify them as potential manifestations of a new type of human being.

The New Man

In this case, Leni Pfeiffer, a woman, is an individual with inherent goodness, compassion and strength. The strength to be herself is perhaps her main quality. She is not aggressive, but she insists on living by her own perspectives. She does not wish to stir up antagonism, like Schnier, whose lack of qualities, such as compassion, contributed to his hyper-aggressiveness. Schnier, in contrast to Leni, Boris, and Lev, generated a social dimension not by his life, but by criticism.

Xenophilia

One of the most promising qualities of Leni, Boris, and Lev is their love of mankind. Leni chooses a Russian for her lover during the Nazi war. Boris loves German poetry; Lev champions the foreign workers in Germany. The specter of nationalism, so dangerous still in Europe and the world, has no meaning to the members of this "Holy Family."

Leni's Irresistibility

The men who know Leni find her very attractive. Pelzer, for example, old man and experienced womanizer that he is, falls hopelessly in love with her, insisting that he has never been in love before. Even the women are somehow not immune to Leni as a sensual creature, since Leni's humanity as such is bound up with her sensuality. All of those who know her well react to her in a fashion that reveals the best in them. Even the Hoysers, whom the "Au" had expected to be sharks of the worst sort, bend over backwards to accommodate Leni. Objectively speaking, i.e., in the framework of their capitalist values, the Hoysers are amazingly deferential to Leni. In their dealing with her, those around her are confronted with their own potentiality as human beings.

Leni As Symbol Of Wholeness

The Nazis among her acquaintances are the most resistant to the effect Leni has on people; yet they use her to mask their unwholesome fanaticism. They declare her the "most German girl in her school." The Communists make use of her as a symbol also. They wish to imply that Leni as the German wife of a Russian indicates things to come in the solidarity of man. Of course, Boris is not chosen by Leni simply because he is a Russian, or a Communist. Mahmet, her last lover in the book, is a Turk.

Social Criticism

Mainly, Böll's social concern in this novel is directed at the problem of the foreign workers in Germany. Böll chastises his countrymen for isolating these people and for assigning to them the lowest points on the social scale. They tend to be garbage collectors, for example. Böll ties up the treatment of these workers with that of the "foreigners" during the war. Sister Rahel, too, has a connection with waste products. She, too, is an alien, and is kept in virtual imprisonment in her convent.

SYMBOLISM

The Bread

In a twist to the Bible, according to which man does not live by bread alone, Leni seems to live solely by her breakfast rolls. The breaking of bread, as has been pointed out earlier in this study guide, is a communal, even sacramental act in Böll's works. In order to partake of it, Leni endures great abuse when she ventures from her apartment to buy her rolls. The bread especially, but also the entire interest in this novel in the physical, the material, is a reflection of Böll's desire to create a new dimension, which he has called, the "sacrality of the material."

Reproductions Of Human Organs

In terms of dualistic Christian thinking, the body is mere matter, even sinful. That aspect of the **metaphysical**, from whose vantage point the body is placed in such an abominably negative position, is revealed as empty in Böll's thinking. But when the spiritual is manifest in the physical, as another perspective of Christian thought has it, as for example in the sacrament of marriage, which is valid only if two become one flesh, the offensive duality disappears. The spiritual then is no longer empty or abstract. It is immanent in the physical. Thus the greater the concern for the physical, in terms of Leni's reverence for it, the purer is the individual's attitude. Therefore the biological charts, magnifying the human organs, including those of reproduction, and the biological charts on Leni's walls, symbolize Leni's unorthodox mentality.

Retina Of Rahel Haruspica's Left Eye

The eye as an organ reveals the fantastic magnitude of a physical phenomenon. It involves a staggering effort of nature, the creation of millions of rods and cones. Leni's intent to paint a cross-section of one layer of Rahel's eye shows her reverence for the wonders of the human body. By painting Rahel's eye, Leni pays tribute to the person who taught her to appreciate the miracle of physicality.

Idyll In The Ruins

Somehow the idyll in the ruins, including Leni, Boris, Lev, and assorted intimates should have germinated into a better Germany than the one that actually rose from the ashes. The idyll, all hope and potentiality, is not much more than a dream of what might have been. Lev, this signal of a new beginning, is "born among corpses" but winds up in jail as a young man although he is anything but a criminal. Leni's public repute could not be worse; when the novel begins, her circumstances are nearly desperate. But Böll seems to indicate the possibilities for a second chance. Through the efforts of the "Au," all of Leni's friends regenerate their concern for Leni and, with their efforts, Leni's significance increases. Since they are all somewhat better people for knowing Leni, her crisis elicits very positive human responses in them. They form a collective to help her and a new, brief idyll ensues. There is laughter and congeniality as they celebrate having averted Leni's eviction. The symbol of this idyll of camaraderie is certainly not as compelling as the one in the burial vaults. It is more to indicate that there is always some room for hope for the renewal of a communal spirit. But its chances are greatest at truly auspicious moments in history, like at the collapse of the Nazi empire. It does not follow here that Böll is advocating Communism, although there is repeated reference to the idyll among the ruins as the "Soviet Paradise." The term is indicative of a possibility for a new communal life, not as an option on Böll's part for Soviet Communism. The paradise is as much Christian as it is Communist. The refusal of the Russians in the novel to return to their homeland after the war is a clear indication that Russia is anything but a place of paradise.

STRUCTURE

On first glance, there seem to be some structural similarities between Group *Portrait with Lady* and *Billiards at Half-Past Nine*. In both novels, the events are illuminated in a multiple perspective. But the goals of the investigation are quite different in the two works. In the earlier novel, the investigation principally concerns the events and the characters' reaction to them. In *Group Portrait with Lady*, one character, Leni Pfeiffer, and the reaction to her by the characters around her are the object of the search. Whereas the narrator in *Billiards at Half-Past Nine* manipulated the information as he saw fit, the "Au" in *Group Portrait with Lady* is a reporter interested only in factual information. Böll does well to reduce the narrator to this status in this novel, for the information he gathers, although largely factual, we presume, borders on hagiography. Leni is called "almost perfect" and "the human-divine Leni." These epithets reveal the reason for the "Au's" project, the portraiture of Leni: His search arises from the hope of finding a being whose integrity is intact, whose individualism is inviolate, a real person who is at once a symbol for the potential incorruptibility of the human individual. At one point, Leni's dual role as symbol and person is referred to in terms of a paradoxical entity: "She exists, and yet she doesn't. She doesn't exist, and yet she does." The search is objective, but also to verify a hope, and this hope may shape objectivity. Thus the image of Leni exists from the start; it merely needs developing. We find practically all essentials about her in nude on the first fifty pages of the novel.

It is significant that the "Au" does not make great efforts to approach Leni directly. He thereby reduces his own importance and increases his credibility. Leni therefore emerges as defined by a great number of people, i.e., in a social dimension. If Leni's portrait is to have an effect, it must be a "group portrait."

As the portrait of Leni gains profile throughout the book, the "Au" and most of his informants become more fascinated with her, for the image they help to create can be of meaning in their own lives. Leni is someone who is not enmeshed in their achievement-oriented society as they are, and she therefore appears to be autonomous to them. Ironically, her financial crisis affects them more than it does her. Her debts do not seem to bother Leni greatly. The thematic structure of the novel, then, is a sort of hagiographic quest for a human being with whom those searching, among them especially the "Au," can identify. For this reason Leni is so super-real and at the same time, an ideal.

The success of the quest in a novel of this type is measured by the success of the created image on those searching. *In Group Portrait with Lady* we can notice a steady increase in involvement, especially of the "Au" with the object of his search. His feelings for Leni become increasingly reverent. The characters involved are brought closer to each other, culminating in the idyll of congeniality of which we spoke.

The trend toward an increased intensity of feeling is mirrored by a gradual increase in the level of the humor in the book. Technically, the quest for Leni as the quintessential, real yet ideal human being is revealed by the tension between the often lackluster, hyper-objective journalistic method of inquiry and reporting - the clumsy abbreviations, the pedantic detail - and the underlying idealistic, humanistic nature of the quest.

LITERARY POINT OF VIEW

The narrator subscribes to an almost painful circumscription of his knowledge. He poses as a journalist and thereby conveys the notion of true objectivity. He heightens it by referring to himself only in the third, not in the first person. All his distance to Leni, however, cannot keep him from becoming one of Leni's fans.

STYLE

If we were to take Böll's style as apart from his thematic concerns, we would have to label it as largely dry, occasionally humorless, journalistic prose. It seems considerably more awkward than that of *Billiards at Half-Past Nine* and *The Clown*. One qualification must be added, however. As has been said, the "Au" becomes increasingly involved with Leni. The style reflects this. It becomes more humorous toward the end of the book. The English translation tends to heighten the negative aspects of the style, probably because on the whole American journalistic prose is even drier than its German equivalent. The American reviewer in Time referred to the novel as "stillborn" fiction. Admittedly, especially the first 150 some pages could warrant such a charge.

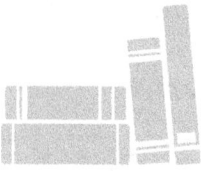

GROUP PORTRAIT WITH LADY

COMMENTARY

Group Portrait with Lady is Böll's most ambitious novel to date. Not only is it his longest, but his attempt to create a realistic character with the somewhat mythic dimensions that Leni manifests has to be admired for its boldness. In our age, the literary hero is more likely to be like Kafka's *Hunger Artist*, who cannot help being "heroic," but would love to be like everyone else. Leni, of course, is no martyr. She may suffer, since she is human, but her sense of self is intact. In Leni, Böll returns to the traditional Aristotelian hero who reflects a higher potential in man, not merely an interesting variant from the average.

Although there can be no doubt that Böll had been in the running for the Nobel Prize for some time, he received it after the publication of *Group Portrait with Lady*. The laudatio singled this novel out among his many achievements. It has been said that Böll received the Nobel Prize as much for the humanistic ethos in his oeuvre as for his literary skills. There can be no doubt that Leni is Böll's most rigorous attempt to date at defining the humanistic possibilities in man. It may be the very rigor of his portrayal, however, that makes this novel less satisfactory to this reader than *The Clown*, or even *Billiards at Half-Past Nine*.

GROUP PORTRAIT WITH LADY

CHARACTER ANALYSES

The cast of characters in *Group Portrait with Lady* is as huge as that in some Russian novels. Unlike Böll himself, the translator into English has given the reader some valuable help by listing the characters as a preface to the novel.

LENI

Leni is the culmination in Böll's work of his search for a heroic figure in our age. With Leni, Böll overcomes the weaknesses of Schnier, her precursor in some respects, creating an entirely viable, although unique human being. Leni, like Schnier, is a misfit in their achievement-directed society. But whereas Schnier cannot live by his sense of self alone, Leni has the strength to do so. Her instincts and intuitions contradict and expose the values of her society as inferior. Simply by being herself, Leni manages to become not only the object of a search for individuality among those who know her well, but she also functions as a bonding factor in their relationships with one another and in their quest for a sense of self.

PELZER

Pelzer has been an opportunist all his life. With an unerring instinct for survival, he manages to exploit every situation. His opportunism is coupled with a certain "humanity." He recognizes that it pays to help people when the risk is not too great. But Pelzer receives his just desserts. His egotistical self-sufficiency breaks down in his old age. Leni causes him, who has been a ladies' man all his life, to fall hopelessly in love for the first time. The perennial exploiter becomes the exploited, not by Leni, but by his own recognition that he is on the losing side of a relationship.

MARIE

Marie is the prostitute with the golden heart and somewhat of an embarrassment to the reader's credulity. Her liaisons are depicted as unobjectionable because she consorts with men to relieve their needs. As a result, she contracts syphilis. Böll has said that he was especially fascinated with Marie and that he would like to expand the character further. In a different dimension, she is as far-fetched as Leni. She remains pure, in spite of her life, and is killed not by her disease, as one might presume, but by blushing to death over the obscenities with which the people in the hospital taunt her.

THE "AU"

The "Au" is the narrator as well as a character in the novel. Though he is a pedantic and stubborn sort, he is nonetheless quite an engaging character. He is a chain smoker (like Böll) and will smoke anywhere, even if he knows it is frowned upon.

There are concrete points of contact in his affinity with Leni. As Leni will do most anything to keep her beloved piano, the "Au" goes to great lengths to restore his old jacket which the Hoysers have damaged. Leni's social and sensual dimensions seem to have a beneficial effect on him. He kisses a nun and establishes a liaison with her after she leaves her order.

HERBERT GRUYTENS

Herbert Gruytens, Leni's father, shows character traits we find in Leni. He, too, is interested neither in power nor any ideology. He is his own person. On the surface, however, it seems that he is a superb achiever in his society. But he merely plays at being successful and has no commitment to his business. He makes it a game to outwit the Nazi production machine, but gets into trouble when he staffs a non-existing company with names from Russian literature. Returning from jail, he makes no effort whatever to regain an elevated position in post-war Germany and dies in an accident because he is really quite incompetent at anything that does not call upon his sense of play.

BÖLL'S SHORT STORIES: SATIRIC

MY UNCLE FRED (1951)

INTRODUCTION

Even more so than in English translation, the **satires** are characterized in German by a specific tone of narration. Some lack completely, and others in part, the pathos of moral intensity we found in the non-satiric short stories. They also involve humor in some form. It is most easily recognized when it is situational, as when Bur-Molottke sweats away, intoning "Thou higher Being whom we revere," or when Uncle Ford characterizes the German army's interest in his waste products. The humor of style is very subtle in Böll's satires; it is all but lost in translation. But the humor in the **metaphors** sometimes does come through in translation, as for example in "Action Will Be Taken," where the waitresses are "full of unsung songs, like chickens of unlaid eggs," or, in the same story, when the hero runs the phrase "action will be taken" through its many modes and inflections. Of course, all this does not mean that the **satires** have no serious purpose. The undeniable aim of satire is to attack and redress something; the satirist's aim is moral. It has been indicated in this study guide that Böll has a penchant for moral explicitness. In the satires, he has found the form that renders his moral pathos inoffensive and yet does not in the slightest distract from the moral aim.

In order to score his moral points clearly and yet avoid sentimentality, Böll employs several devices characteristic of **satire**: Exaggeration - The **protagonist** in "This is Tibten" has not one, but two Ph.D.'s, and has attended five universities to prepare himself for saying, "Here is Tibten." Comic Grotesqueness - In "Action Will Be Taken" someone knits with his feet while answering the phone and writing with a pen in his mouth, exemplifying the senseless activity in Wunsiedel's factory. Absurdity - The **protagonist** in "The Thrower-Away" turns wastefulness into an ideological formula in order to save. Aestheticized Aggression - The thrust of the satirist is aggressive. But in order to show that the satiric purpose is not destructive, but correctional, the satirist takes pains to transform the aggressive dimension. In "Murke's Collected Silences," the offensive member is cut up symbolically; in "Action Will Be Taken," he is killed by a momentary inactivity.

MY UNCLE FRED

As in *Tomorrow and Yesterday*, Böll here is concerned with a world without fathers. The narrator of the story, then a boy, was thrust into the role of the provider. Naturally, he welcomes the return of his Uncle Fred from the war. Contrary to everyone's expectations, Uncle Fred does nothing for a while but eat, smoke, and sleep, making it very questionable that he will be a good provider and relieve the boy of his burdens of procuring food on the black market.

RESPONSIBILITY

Uncle Fred is indeed a questionable provider. He is good in the economic sense, as it turns out, but a washout as a provider of values to the boy. If Uncle Fred would have had a sense of values, he would have been concerned with two overriding facts: the war, and the black market. When asked about the war, he refuses to discuss it save the fact that the army had the audacity to make him urinate in a bottle upon induction. This, and not the senseless destruction of lives, or questions of guilt and involvement, made him distrust the military. On the topic of the black market, Uncle Fred is the only person with whom the boy can discuss these problems without getting into an argument. Uncle Fred, then, sees nothing wrong with the boy's involvement in it.

Thus Uncle Fred does not provide the guidance the boy needs. He is a surrogate father who gives the boy surrogate values. He teaches him how to get on economically, not ethically.

SURROGATE VALUES

The nature of Uncle Fred's business is the link to the social dimension of the **satire**. He becomes an extremely successful flower merchant. Why, we may ask, should flowers sell so well after a war, when money is needed for food and shelter? The answer is quite simple. Flowers cover up the scars of the war, be they the ruins of the cities or the consciences of the people. The fact is that for many Germans the post-war era was not a period of moral reconstruction, but of the "economic miracle." Inwardly impoverished, they turned to fine clothing, tasteful homes, elegant cars as a means of compensation. In "Murke's Collected Silences," good taste is a fetish to everyone. The ashtrays in the elevators are so artistic that no one dares to use them. The Germans, there can be no doubt, to a large degree shifted their values from ethics to esthetics.

SYMBOLS OF SHIFT TO ESTHETICS

The flowers are the first symbol of the shift. The second is Fred's answer to the war questions. He rejects them because the "German Reich" (Typically, he uses a euphemism for the Nazi period. The concept goes back to the Middle Ages when it had an idealistic meaning.) exhibited bad taste when it made him urinate into a bottle. The third is Uncle Fred on the sofa, where he lounges idyllically, crumbling bread onto his tongue like some decadent ancient popping grapes into his mouth. More telling even is his reaction to the sofa. He does not like it because he objects to the terrible pink of its material. For this reason he rails against his forebears who bought the sofa, calling them "stuffy," and "constipated owls." The fourth symbolic indication of the shift is Fred's looks. He is described as having the appearance of a marble statue. Instead of a person, he is something from the realm of esthetics. Lest we mistake this description of Fred as a compliment, Böll likens him to a "damaged" statue.

STUNTED CONSCIOUSNESS

The narrator tells the story as an adult. He does not seem to understand the shift from true to surrogate values connected with Uncle Fred. He still likes Uncle Fred, for he is the only person who makes his "memories of the years after 1945 bearable." The narrator's conscience obviously still troubles him about his youthful involvement in the black market, but Fred and his flowers have provided an effective pain suppressant, although they have not eliminated the cause of the pain. There is no recognition in the narrator, and Böll implies that, in his countrymen in general, the moral problems connected with the war must be faced squarely and directly.

THE MOTHER

Böll, as has been indicated before, likes to provide the exception along with the general rule. The mother of the narrator is the exception here. She has not lost her sense of right and wrong, for every time her little son goes off to the black market, she has tears in her eyes. Knowing what people ought to be concerned about, she feels that flowers will not sell right after the war. She overestimates her fellow human beings and, of course, is wrong.

Comment

This story, humorous, tongue-in-cheek, biting, yet apparently harmless, is one of the most effective **satires** in German literature on the refusal of most Germans to implicate themselves in the war guilt. The subtlety of the story, one may assume, must have precluded the point from being generally understood in Germany. But those who did not understand it probably could not have been persuaded to understand themselves anyway. Böll makes this point in "This is Tibten," to be discussed next.

BÖLL'S SHORT STORIES: SATIRIC

THIS IS TIBTEN (1953)

The **protagonist** in this story is very much on the defensive. He complains that "heartless people" are at a loss to understand why he, a man who has earned two Ph. D.'s and attended five universities, should spend his life announcing "This is Tibten" to trains arriving at the Tibten station.

IRRESPONSIBLE INTELLECTUAL

The **protagonist** is equipped by training and insight to tell his fellow men about "the wisdom of the world," but instead his contribution to society exhausts itself in the announcement that passengers have arrived in Tibten.

WISDOM OF THE WORLD

The **protagonist** knows what it is. He understands that the animals of the Roman boy are toys, not some kind of chess figures, as a historical authority interprets the pieces. The boy who died because of a girl he could not have was but a child, still playful and innocent, not someone addicted to a "war game." The wisdom of the world, which the **protagonist** understands, is tragic wisdom. It is the incommensurability of the world of the child with its **connotations** of innocence and beauty and the world of adults associated with the ugly facts of existence that take priority over such things as love. Significantly, the boy is sent by his father to Germany on business on an adult mission. He is to buy lead. The child's world, then, symbolic of beauty, playfulness and innocence, is crushed.

PROBLEM OF EVIL

The wisdom of the world is in the final analysis the recognition of the problem of evil. Böll here in this story works entirely without a Christian frame of reference, possibly because his **protagonist** is an educated man, i. e., a person whose moral frame of reference is humanistic, traceable to secular cultural roots, the classical Greek and Roman heritage.

PROTAGONIST'S ALIBI

The **protagonist**, then, is a man who should alert the tourists to the real meaning of the grave of Tiburtius. But he does not. The **protagonist** is the target of the satiric attack. He is a cop-out. Ideally seen, instead of intoning "This is Tibten," he should be shouting from the rooftops about the meaning of Tiburtius' death. However, the **protagonist** does not live in an ideal world and we cannot condemn him. He has a rather valid excuse: Very few would understand him or take him seriously. And those who would understand would not need to be shouted at from the rooftops. Thus he modulates his announcements at the station "so that those who are asleep do not wake up, and those who are awake will not fail to hear me, and I put just enough enticement in my voice, that those who are dozing rouse themselves and wonder if Tibten was not their destination."

PROTAGONIST AND WRITER

The protagonist's function bears a resemblance to that of the writer. "This is Tibten" is to a considerable degree self-satire. The writer, like the **protagonist**, must not shout his moral credo from the rooftops. The writer, too, must modulate his tones so that those who are inclined and equipped to listen, will indeed listen. The satirist is a moralist, to be sure, but he is not a preacher. Esthetic concerns must be primary. This, of course, places him in a dilemma, into a situation that warrants confession as well as self-justification.

PERILS OF THE DILEMMA

The **protagonist** seems to be presumptuous. To prove that no one else understands the real significance of the animals from Tiburtius' grave, he substitutes those he received along with his margarine purchases. He is right, no one can tell the difference between the authentic and the fake animals. Obviously he should now feel moved to heed his role as the one and only individual who could enlighten the tourists at Tiburtius' grave. But he does not do anything of the sort. Instead, he continues in his attempts to insist that his work at the station is indeed not beneath his dignity. In the final analysis, however, the **protagonist** is the fool. He himself is now incapable of differentiating between Tiburtius' animals and the margarine toys which he had put in the same drawer. In terms of the writer's role, the dilemma is likely to be a permanent one: As a writer he must mix ethics and esthetics so that they form a homogeneous entity; as a man he must not lose sight of the difference, for one does not relate to human beings through art primarily.

DECADENCE

Although some of the lady visitors at Tiburtius' grave shed a few sentimental tears, the grave has primarily historical, or, worse, commercial value as a tourist attraction. It is far from anything that could teach "the wisdom of the world," to which the inscription of the grave points: "He was but a boy, yet love was his undoing." The motif of decadence, of a loss of value, is echoed by a significant detail: The Roman boy is sent on a trip whose purpose is business and thus should be undertaken by an adult only. The purpose is to buy lead which, as some historians hold, was primarily used in Roman waterpipes and drinking vessels, causing a gradual but ultimately debilitating lead-poisoning in Roman society.

Comment

As Böll chastises the intellectual for shirking his duty as a guide and teacher, he insists on an important qualification. The literary satirist is limited in his effectiveness as a moral guide by the dictates of his craft. He cannot let it degenerate into preaching. On the other hand, he cannot suppress the moral aim of his work to the point where it is no longer recognizable. It is a difficult and delicate balancing act that he must perform. The juggler may very easily look the fool in it.

BÖLL'S SHORT STORIES: SATIRIC

ACTION WILL BE TAKEN (1954)

One of the ideals of Western societies has been the active man. The ideal, generated by the Greeks and brought to us during the Renaissance, implies that the significant individual interacts with his environment in actively constructive terms. Goethe's Faust ends his life on this note. He is an engineer, reclaiming land from the sea.

ACTION FOR ACTION'S SAKE

In this story, Böll sees the ideal of action as having lost its meaning in the modern world. It has become an empty value. Action is something we do for its own sake, no matter, how silly or futile it is: "Don't just stand there, for heaven's sake, do something, anything." The purpose of all the action in Wunsiedel's factory never becomes clear to the **protagonist**. He does not really know what the factory produces.

MODES OF MEANINGLESS ACTION

This **satire** is no doubt one of Böll's most humorous. The secretary who is a graduate in psychology, a marathon knitter, a breeder of dogs, and a nightclub singer is as funny as Broschek who operates a knitting-machine with his feet while he telephones and works a pen with his mouth.

SELF-DECEIT

The action at Wunsiedel's factory does not go unrecognized as being meaningless. Broschek for one shows that he has not lost the faculty for distinguishing between significant and useless action. When the protagonist announces Wunsiedel's death by saying that there has been some action, Broschek knows immediately that something serious has taken place. He spits out the pen, puts down the two telephone receivers, and stops knitting with his feet. The people in the factory, then, know how senseless their activities are; yet they pursue them.

ACCOMMODATED HERO

The **protagonist** knows clearly from the beginning that he is compromising himself in Wunsiedel's factory. His excuse is that he must eat. But he jumps on the "Action must be taken" bandwagon with such fervor that we must fault him for being a phony. It seems, however, that he can escape Wunsiedel's factory and the world of pointless action. He becomes a professional mourner. When Böll has Wunsiedel fall dead across the doorway, obstructing the exit, he indicates that the **protagonist** is caught. Although he steps over the corpse, he does not really free himself from Wunsiedel's world of senseless work. As a professional mourner he is no longer hyperactive, to be sure, but his work is not much more meaningful. A professional mourner does not really grieve, he goes through the motions of mourning. That our protagonist occasionally dresses up the funerals of the poor by his presence does not alter that fact. The protagonist's big chance for some sensible action was to expose the reasons for Wunsiedel's death. When his boss is dead, he says, "We must take action." At this juncture, the phrase is pregnant with potentiality. But instead of a call for reform, the **protagonist** permits it to be a call for Wunsiedel's burial. The **protagonist** simply mourns the world, he makes no attempt to change it. Thus he is drawn into the satiric focus, and rightfully so since he has a natural propensity for being a critic of purposeless action. He is a pensive man. But he prostitutes his gift of thought. He does not use it; he wears it like a badge, looking not like the thinker he is, but like the mourner others want him to be. Thus he accommodates himself within his society. No wonder the death of Wunsiedel is seen by him as a positive event. It helped him discover his true vocation as a mourner.

CLEANLINESS, GOOD TASTE, CHEERFULNESS

Böll spoofs all these bourgeois values. People are filled with good cheer and enthusiasm to the bursting point, while they should be thoughtful and subdued by the state of affairs. The immense and hectic process of production is pointless; it promotes sterility in human relationships. The soap the **protagonist** supposes to be the factory's product seems to point to this notion. Equally offensive in this context is the all-pervading good taste in the factory's appointments. The esthetic dimension - as in "My Uncle Fred," and "Murke's Collected Silences," to be discussed next - helps to cover up deficiencies in the humanistic dimension.

Comment

This is probably the zaniest of Böll's satires. In being funnier here than in most of his other stories, Böll pays heed to the exigencies of his topic and **theme**. Action, motion, tend to be more comical then inactivity. The story loses much of its humor when the **protagonist** becomes a mourner.

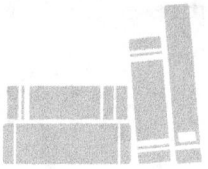

BÖLL'S SHORT STORIES: SATIRIC

MURKE'S COLLECTED SILENCES (1955)

....

It has been claimed that the object of Böll's attack is the radio industry. If this were true, if this **satire** were an expose of the news media as opinion manipulators, Böll would have included the perspective of a manipulated audience. We do meet one listener, Jadwiga Herchen, who wants a feature about the canine soul. But this lady is anything but a manipulated listener. In fact, she threatens the radio company and succeeds in having her ridiculous suggestion taken seriously. Her name is significant in this connection. It means "little master." The listening public is indeed in charge to a considerable degree.

CONSUMER AS DICTATOR

The broadcasting industry in Germany, similar to its American counterpart, provides that which the consumer demands. But more so than on the consumer one could focus on the prevailing spirit of the times, on its taste, as the dictatorial force. The individual shapes and changes his beliefs and views according to this force. Bur-Malottke is servile to public taste which at present prefers to ignore religious concerns. Bur-Malottke in turn rules the hierarchy of the broadcasting company. "One simply does not contradict him."

PRINCIPLE OF POWER

Clearly, Bur-Malottke is the offensive member in the story. He is the dominant ape and since his person is undoubtedly the direct target of the satirist's ridicule, the principle for which he stands is the object of the **satire**. Bur-Malottke represents a man who is totally aligned with the principle of dominance and submission, the hierarchical order of rank and power. It is this principle that underlies West German society as probably all other major societies in the world. But it is not a positive principle, for it seems to corrupt everyone, including Murke. If this principle - ultimately a reflection of man's aggressive nature - is inherent in social life as we know it, the only possible way of dealing with it is to attach it to worthwhile causes, to sublimate aggression, to turn it into beneficial social impulses. This is precisely what Bur-Malottke purports to do. He pretends to be an intellectual whose function is to enlighten everyone. He anchors his views, like that on art as an absolute. But he is a phony. He relativizes the absolute. After the war, it is God; later it is the "higher Being whom we revere." Obviously, Bur-Malottke is rather worthless, but he is a true representative of his society in which the individual has one ultimate value: He wishes to rise to the top in the stratifications of power.

EXCEPTIONAL INDIVIDUAL

There are two categories of people who are, or could be, exceptions. There are Murke's mother who prays for him, the good-natured and simple waitress Wulla, and Murke's girlfriend who feels the indignity in being subjected to Murke's demands for silence. The role these women play in the story largely explains their exceptional status. They are not part of the hierarchy. Potential exceptions are the writers who insist vociferously that they are interested in art above all, but only one of them admits that his involvement in the radio company corrupts him. But even he eagerly serves Moloch. The only other significant exception among the men seems to be Murke.

SATIRIC STRUCTURE

Satiric structure tends to mimic that which it wishes to expose. The thrower-away's formula - in the **satire** to be discussed next - mimics the capitalist formula; the **protagonist** in "This is Tibten" has the same unconcern for "the wisdom of the world" that he sees in the tourists. The phenomenon can be reduced to the similarity between the accuser and the accused, threat and counterthreat, in terms of the perspective of control of power. In satire, there is the challenger and the challenged. The challenger initially has right on his side. But since he wishes to prevail, to persuade, he exercises power and he inadvertently becomes part of that which he had set out to defeat. For what makes the challenged so odious is the fact that false, or outworn, or misused ideas are maintained by power. The challenger's initial strength is the purity of ideas vis a vis the hollowness of those of the challenged who maintain them by force. The challenger, unfortunately for him, can usually be effective only by meeting them with power himself, the use of which is then his undoing. The structure of "Murke's Collected Silences" is a textbook example of this mechanism typical of much satire.

PATERNOSTER ELEVATOR

Riding the contraption is a need for Murke. It is his "anxiety breakfast." The elevator is a symbol for climbing the ladder in the corporate hierarchy. It has the same functions as Murke's dreams. He is afraid of this climb, especially of the moment at the top, before the elevator descends again. In the symbolic sense the top is where Bur-Malottke is, a frightening position indeed. The paternoster elevator uses the principle of the wheel; it goes round and round in an endless cycle. The circular pattern devalues the notion of the rise. Bur-Malottke will be replaced someday. The moment at the top is brief.

CHALLENGE

Murke shows that Bur-Malottke is despicable. But instead of attacking him for his intellectual and moral charlatanism, he uses Bur-Malottke's own weapons on him. Murke is equipped to deal with Bur-Malottke. He is chosen by the director for the task Bur-Malottke wants performed because he is an "intellectual wild animal." He does submit Bur-Malottke to a humiliating experience, not in terms of Bur-Malottke's charlatanism, however, but in terms of the patterns of dominance and submission. When Murke begins to collect silences he does so in order to counteract the meaningless verbiage connected with his work. It is a symbolic protest. Once he has faced Bur-Malottke, however, he has met the moment of truth. From then on collecting silences is no longer a legitimate form of protest. In fact, it is definable in the perspective of dominance and submission. When Murke makes his girl record silences for him, he exercises power over her. By his own admission, his girl is nice. She is the kind of girl the simple Wulla wishes him to have as an antidote to his work. Murke's girl senses what Murke is doing to her. She finds it immoral. Murke is no longer the enemy of empty verbiage. He now is interested in power. Thus he does not mind taking his girl to the movies, where he will be barraged with sound. But there the patterns of dominance and submission are not involved, as they are when he is alone with his girl. He even subjects her to the indignity of having to ask permission to speak.

ROLE OF RELIGION

Religion provides the fixed point of reference in Bur-Malottke's and Murke's jungle - but only for the reader. Murke sticks the religious picture he received from his mother on some door so that there is at least one "corny picture" among all the exquisitely tasteful furnishings in the building. But by this very act Murke reveals that he senses the phoniness of the place. Here, as in "My Uncle Fred," esthetics replace ethics.

Bur-Malottke cuts out the word God from his speeches, and several of the people in the story use the word God is a context in which it has no religious meaning whatever. The drama director and even the author of the atheist play find that silence is too obtrusive an answer to the question about the meaninglessness of existence, and they simply splice in the word God which had been cut out of Bur-Malottke's speech. But God and religion nonetheless seem to have a way of prevailing, not only in the atheist play, but also in the end, so to speak. The story concludes with the technician reading out the words under the "corny picture": "I prayed for you at St. James Church."

Comment

Although we are familiar with the individual who gains the world and loses his soul in several of Böll's stories, "Murke's Collected Silences" treats the **theme** more compellingly than the others. It employs some comic effects, but in comparison with the other **satires** discussed it is very serious. However, the story is never sentimental. The sparsity of comic neutralization of the satiric thrust in this piece seems to be an asset. Among the **satires** of Böll, "Murke's Collected Silences" is undoubtedly the most moving, and possibly the best.

BÖLL'S SHORT STORIES: SATIRIC

THE THROWER-AWAY (1957)

The **protagonist** is a saver by inclination. As a boy he had collected travel brochures and he has retained the saver's frame of mind as an adult. He wishes to save human resources by eliminating "junk mail." Through his throw-away efforts he attacks the capitalist system. Where he seemingly saves, he accelerates the consumption of resources and thereby hastens the arrival of the moment when resources will be depleted. Thus, by accentuating the principle of consumption, he exposes the capitalist doctrine that holds that wealth is created through stimulated consumption. Though written in 1957, this **satire** is obviously immensely timely in the point it makes.

PROTAGONIST'S DILEMMA

The thrower-away is a happy man as long as he is not socially and economically integrated. But since he needs to eat, he must work, and in a real situation his throw-away formula, so logical and humanitarian in theory, turns into a two-edged sword. The **protagonist** finds himself an accomplice in the capitalist system. While he saves, he actually wastes things.

Furthermore, the economic establishment confuses him when an insurance company adopts his formula, whereas other firms had rejected it as "asocial." When Böll makes the company which likes his formula an insurance company, he indicates that the protagonist's quandary is not essentially confined to him. An insurance company's raison d'etre is social; its principle is humanitarian. But in actuality, it is not a pure endeavor. The profit motive is involved and thus the underlying principle is compromised much as the thrower-away's ideas lose their luster in the real world. The thrower-away's confusion takes its toll. He needs tranquilizers and he feels he must mask himself as an average citizen.

PROTAGONIST'S SOCIETY

When Böll speaks of the thrower-away making efforts to appear as a man "deeply rooted in the principles of democracy," he is ironic. Democracy, i.e., concepts of equality, humanitarianism, etc., seems to play no great role in this society. It is not mainly democratic, but capitalist, i.e., competitive, and, as Böll sees it, primitive. He indicates this by linking competitiveness with militarism and even with the Nazis. The common denominator is the notion of the survival of the fittest. Capitalism promotes the notion in the economic; Nazism promoted it in the biological realm. But there are distinctions to be made, and Böll makes them. Fascism is more primitive than capitalism. Thus the **protagonist** finds himself explaining the difference to his fellow citizens who think the SA (Hitler's brown-shirts) are the same as the U.S.A. (the prototypical capitalist country to the Germans). Furthermore, his fellow Germans find cheer in the joke told every morning at the Schlieffen-Street tram stop. Schlieffen was the German general who designed the attack plans for the Western front during World War I. (This **episode** was omitted by the translator in *18 Stories*. Unfortunately, but understandably so, since the reference would be lost on many American readers). Another tram stop is Roon-Street, the name of another German general and minister of war.

SATIRIC CHALLENGER

The thrower-away **refrains** from an all-out attack on the system as such. He has a correctional rather than revolutionary aim. Thus he is still to a degree in sympathy with his society. Being in part in, and in part out of it, confuses him. He works for and against the system and as a result he looks somewhat ridiculous.

Comment

This piece can be considered one of Böll's finest satires. Upon close examination, it yields numerous brilliant points scored on German post-war society and on capitalism in general. The texture of the narrative is very dense. Every nuance - they obviously cannot all be discussed here - contributes to the satiric theme.

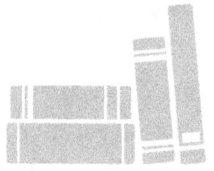

BÖLL'S SHORT STORIES: NON-SATIRIC

THE DEATH OF ELSA BASKOLEIT (1951)

Böll has repeatedly indicated that he has a special affinity with the short story. He has written some sixty stories to date, and he intends to write more. About twenty of them are unalloyed masterpieces. There exists one anthology of his short fiction in English, *18 Stories*, translated by Leila Vennewitz (McGraw-Hill, 1966). This anthology contains several of Böll's best stories, and those analyzed here are all contained in it. The criterion for selection was somewhat subjective; however, those chosen for discussion are by and large the pieces that are most frequently anthologized in Germany. The short stories have been widely translated, though it can be said that Böll's prestige outside of Germany rests largely on his novels.

Many of Böll's stories are **satire**, and they are all in all his best efforts. In *18 Stories*, six are unquestionably satiric. They are all excellent and [five] are selected here for analysis. Of the non-satiric pieces, four are selected for discussion.

"THE DEATH OF ELSA BASKOLEIT"

We never learn of the physical cause for Elsa Baskoleit's death, and we know that it is not important. We do sense, however, that in the world with which Böll confronts us in this story, her death seems almost merciful.

VICTIMIZATION OF CHILDREN

Elsa Baskoleit wishes to become a dancer. She practices in tights and before a window. In consequence, the child is labeled a whore by the narrow-minded and cruel neighbors. The death of Elsa, is, figuratively speaking, the fault to the adults around her who will not tolerate the grace and beauty the child Elsa exemplifies.

LOSS OF CHILDHOOD

The loss of childhood that Elsa's death represents is shown in its effect on the **protagonist**. Adulthood places him in a grey, hopeless, mechanical world. He is a truck driver, the only thing at which he can succeed. Years after having moved away from the neighborhood, he hears the name Baskoleit as he picks up some fruit crates at the wholesaler's. He is moved to drive his truck to Baskoleit's grocery store. Where in his youth his neighborhood was filled with playing children, he now sees but one sullen child, drawing lines in the dust. Baskoleit's store is now a sour-smelling, decaying place, and Baskoleit stands half-crazy behind the counter and, although Elsa has been dead for years, he informs his customers time and again that his daughter has died.

Böll's bleak view of adults as cruel is not dogmatic. Böll rarely makes a blanket condemnation against anyone in his works. He insists on the exception.

SURVIVAL OF CHILDHOOD

Elsa's father, though a gruff man, was a friend of children in the protagonist's youth. "At the bottom of his heart, Baskoleit was a cheerful man. This we knew as surely as only children can know, that his gruffness was a game." Baskoleit as an adult had maintained a sense of play. He tosses the apples and oranges he gives to the children as if they were "rubber balls." This affinity with children, we can surmise, makes him so vulnerable that he can survive the death of his daughter only in a demented state.

EMPATHY AND SHAME

When the **protagonist** leaves Baskoleit's store, he finds the lone child he had seen in the neighborhood standing on the running-board of his truck, reaching into the cab and playing with the blinker controls. Seeing the driver, the boy tries to run away. This **episode** repeats, mutatis mutandis, the essentials of the relationship of the adults to Elsa. What is play, done in all innocence, the adults consider punishable behavior. The adult world, on the other hand, is approached with guileless fascination by the child. But the truckdriver has understood what the death of Elsa Baskoleit means. He grabs the boy, not to punish him for tinkering with his truck, but to give the amazed child an apple from his truck and, as if to make up for Elsa's death, he then gives him more and more apples, finally even stuffing them under the boy's jacket.

One of the two women the **protagonist** sees in Baskoleit's store cries, indicating that the understanding of Elsa's death is not totally lost on the people in the neighborhood. Although Baskoleit's store is a foul-smelling, unpleasant place, and in spite of the fact that he subjects his customers to his constant complaints about his daughter's death, she buys from him. She submits to the ordeal because it is an act of repentance. The scouring powder she buys symbolizes her shame. The other woman in the store, of course, has made herself immune to the meaning of Elsa's death. Tapping her forehead, she indicates that she thinks of Baskoleit as simply crazy, never minding the causes.

Comment

Although the predominant colors of this story are gloomy, Böll blends in highlights that make this one of his more hopeful pieces. With admirable sparseness, he tells us why the transition to adulthood is so often a loss. Play, so crucial to the child, cannot be tolerated by the adult world. Play is devoid of that dreadful seriousness the adults often confuse with a sense of responsibility, and it is therefore immoral and must be punished.

BÖLL'S SHORT STORIES: NON-SATIRIC

THE BALEK SCALES (1952)

The **theme** of the story is social injustice. The Baleks are a combination of feudal landlord and capitalist exploiter. They have set up a law that no one shall own scales, and their command is obeyed without question. The Baleks assumed for themselves the right, and they had the power to enforce this right, to dismiss from their employment those who broke the law, meaning complete ruin to the peasant involved.

This bleak medieval picture contains one positive element. When the Baleks make everyone a gift upon receiving the patent of nobility, they show a trace of the good will that in the early feudal period grew out of the nobility's recognition of the interdependence of the peasants and the aristocracy. Ironically, it is this gift that causes trouble for the Baleks.

DAVID AND GOLIATH

The narrator's grandfather, the **protagonist**, plays the role of the challenger. Then a boy, he is smart, industrious and courageous, and he always carries pebbles for his slingshot with him. Unfortunately, the assault of this David only stuns the Baleks who name themselves "von Bilgan" after a giant who is said to have lived where their house is. Goliath gains the upper hand. In the confrontation between the gendarmes and the villagers, the protagonist's sister is killed and subsequently, the Bruchers are expelled.

Comment

Upon closer analysis, this story, which is one of Böll's most popular, turns out to be one of his weaker efforts. But it is included here for discussion to indicate how uneven in quality Böll's production is.

There can be no doubt that the Balek scales are explicitly symbolic of injustice. However, when we analyze the scales in terms of their precise function in the story, they turn out to be a false **metaphor**. They imply a historically inaccurate consciousness in the peasants and indicate thereby more than anything else Böll's injustice to history. If, we have to ask ourselves, the scales had indeed shown honest weight, would the injustices be done away with? Does that additional 10% of thievery the Baleks perpetrate constitute the essence of the Baleks' injustice to the peasants? Obviously not. If they had given honest weight, the Baleks might not be quite as rich and powerful at the time of the story, but the difference would be slight in view of the fantastic profits they made anyway.

By making the scales the central symbol of social justice - and bracketing out that even honest weight means exploitation - Böll unfortunately deals with a symptom, rather than with an underlying cause. Especially if we are mindful of the pathos with which Böll tells his tale, we have the feeling that he is a physician officiously addressing himself to a cut in the patient's finger while the patient is hemorrhaging inside.

There are further flaws in the story. The time is the turn of the twentieth century. Nonetheless the peasants think and behave as if they lived in the Middle Ages. The smart and tough Brucher family exhaust their reaction to their plight in taking refuge in a religious phrase, "The justice of this earth, O Lord, hath put Thee to death." The phrase implies that the world is not capable of any kind of meaningful justice since it even put Christ to death. It implies further that it is impossible to bring about improved justice for the members of the class to which the Bruchers belong. In view of the fact that Böll wrote the story in the middle of the twentieth century, he must be faulted for having ignored history. The Bruchers of the world have staged revolutions in half the world, toppling the Baleks, and in the other half have gained the right and power to check the scales, and often to readjust them in their own favor.

BÖLL'S SHORT STORIES: NON-SATIRIC

AND THERE WAS THE EVENING AND THE MORNING (1954)

Böll deals here with the first crisis in a marriage. The people involved are extraordinary. The wife no longer speaks to her husband because of one very insignificant lie. The husband knows that most wives would simply counter with their own small lies, realizing that husbands and wives are untruthful to one another now and then. Not so Anna. To her, the lie has severed the bond of trust between her and her husband. Brenig accepts Anna's reaction, for he, too, is a person for whom marriage is a special, even sacred state. The hour between going to bed with Anna and falling asleep is a time of communion, an idyll of harmony and tranquility for him. That it exists, that God created day and night, is to him as wonderful as the creation of "flowers, animals and man."

MARRIAGE AS SACRED COMMUNION

The relationship between husband and wife is here infused by Böll with immense meaning. It is more wondrous than natural creation. In *The Clown*, we recall, Schnier cannot live without Marie. Brenig is similar. The story is full of symbols indicating his loneliness and misery that result from his abject state.

LONELINESS

As he keeps returning to the baggage room at the station for his Christmas gifts to his wife, he sees them flanked by the pieces of luggage of others. One by one, they disappear until his gifts remain alone, "lying on the shelf behind bars as if in prison."

TRANSFORMATION

Brenig's entire outlook on life has changed. The loss of his hour has transformed him. The change is projected by Böll in the events around Brenig. As he walks past the downtown store windows, he sees that the Christmas decorations are being taken down and the windows are redone for the New Year's celebration. Dummies that were angels are transformed instantaneously into bartenders; masks abound. Brenig's changed state is above all reflected in his attitude toward time.

TIME

His expulsion from the paradise of marriage, so to speak, brings about a new consciousness of time as a destructive dimension. His thoughts move from the blissful state of childhood to old age and death. He pictures his wife as a child "dreaming over a book under the lamplight." Then he sees her face as he knows it now, as for a "few moments it would turn to stone." Then he sees it as the face of an old woman. The fear which seizes him now makes him see his own face as old also, "lined with bitterness, worn with suffering." His last vision, tying up with the New Year's decorations in the store windows, is of masks that look like death-heads. His new sense of time issues in the feeling that events of importance have nothing to do with the calendar. They do not fall, he feels, on important calendar days. But Brenig is wrong.

FORGIVENESS AND GRACE

Anna, who gives him a "gay, colorful calendar" for Christmas, still lives in time without the "sting of death." For her, important events on the calendar coincide with important events in life. Although Brenig does not come home until very late on Christmas Eve, she now speaks her first words to him. They are just three, two "no's" and a "yes," but they indicate her forgiveness. The meaning of Christmas as God's supreme expression of grace is alive in her.

MERIT

Brenig, the reader feels, should indeed be forgiven. He has suffered enough for his little lie about his salary. Furthermore, he has retained some redeeming aspects of his former self. He was somewhat of a child and he still is. Among the presents for his wife is a gigantic chocolate piano, a gift selection much more characteristic of a child than of an adult.

RESPONSIBILITY

However, Brenig seems to understand that, in terms of responsibility, his relationship to Anna must now be quite different. He comes to his wife without the presents he has bought for her. Anna has to accept him as he is; she cannot accept bribes. Anna indicates to him that she does not mind at all that he has brought her no gifts.

REBUILDING THE COMMUNION

Acceptance, Böll indicates, does not mean forgetting in the sense of pretending that nothing happened. When Brenig gets home, he finds that Anna has moved the beds apart. But Brenig is sure that his marriage will again have that special hour of communion: "He had regained his hour, had two 'No's,' and a 'Yes,' and when a car came up the street, the headlights made Anna's profile leap up out of the darkness for him."

Comment

Böll fully reveals himself in this story as the moralist he is. But in contrast to some of his works, in which his moral stance is too explicit, he is very subtle and skillful here. The religious framework, though very important here, strikes us as almost coincidental at first. Böll scores his points very subtly. Brenig does not reflect on his plight in specifically religious terms; he does not even remember the exact words of the quote from Genesis that gives the story its title. The "coincidence" of the time being Christmas is so skillfully exploited by Böll that the entire pattern of Brenig's marital crisis is linked to the Christian myth of the loss of paradise and its regaining through grace implicit in Christ's birth.

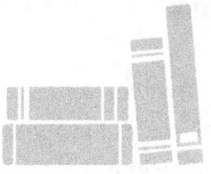

BÖLL'S SHORT STORIES: NON-SATIRIC

LIKE A BAD DREAM (1956)

The unnamed **protagonist** in this story finds himself at a critical juncture in his life. He is confronted with a test of his integrity, and he fails it. The moment of truth comes when he has the opportunity to make a large amount of money by corrupt means. Although he makes a decision, the **protagonist** does not become fully aware of the implications of his choice. His new state of corruption is "beyond understanding" for him. In the larger sense what is beyond understanding, Böll implies, is that a human being chooses corruption even though he can somehow distinguish between right and wrong, and, further, that life is such that everything conspires to trap him into compromising his honesty. "Life," his wife tells the protagonist, "consists of compromises and concessions."

INITIATION RITE

The **protagonist** is prepared by his wife to be initiated into the "real" world, the world of business, the world of "mature" people. The initiation, however, is not a gain, as his wife sees it, but rather a loss. The world changes for the **protagonist**. He looks at his wife differently; she no longer is as attractive to him as before. In the moments following his ordeal, she is not with him. Loneliness is the final note of the story.

RELIGIOUS CONTEXT

The crucifixes, madonnas, the wife's schooling at the nunnery, the mention of Christ, place the references ultimately into a religious context. The protagonist's loss of integrity is to be seen in religious, more specifically, Christian terms. Böll suggests patterns we can associate with the loss of innocence.

SNAKE AND APPLE

The role of woman is that of the temptress. Mrs. Zumpen is a reptilian creature dressed in black pajamas with yellow spots. She makes the protagonist think of lemons. Böll here improves on the Bible. Considering how negative the whole experience is to the **protagonist**, it is no wonder that the fruit of which he tastes is not the traditional apple, but a lemon.

DETERIORATION

The protagonist's corruption is reflected by a note of deterioration in the cultural and historical perspective. To the people in this story, madonnas and crucifixes have no religious meaning. They are merely objects d'art. The protagonist's wife rebukes him for mentioning Christ in connection with money, but then herself suggests that he show Zumpen his crucifix as a pretext for talking to him about the deal. The note of deterioration is delineated further by a sequentiality concerning the madonnas, indicating the loss of religious in favor of artistic values in society. The Zumpens own Gothic, Baroque, "even Rococo Madonnas, if there is such a thing." The **protagonist** is the owner of an eighteenth-century crucifix. Gothic art is associated with extreme religious intensity. The Gothic period is the age of mysticism. In subsequent centuries the religious element diminishes to the point where an eighteenth-century crucifix strikes us as an anomaly, for the eighteenth-century is the age of reason, not of faith.

Comment

The excellence of this story lies in the fact that Böll succeeds in transforming a plight common to nearly every businessman into the essential pattern of an individual's loss of integrity. Böll balances the complicity of the world and the individual's volition in the process of corruption. He furthermore indicates the individual's predilection for corruption, here greed, and his longing to return to his lost, original state. Not yet the full-fledged initiated businessman, the **protagonist** drives through downtown to make the deal at the Zumpens. Having done so, he avoids the business section and instead takes a route past quiet residential areas. He no longer is eager for the world of money that caused his plight, but longs for the world of privacy and non-involvement.

Böll's compassion is with the **protagonist** who, though surrounded by signals that could guide him, is a child of his age which has lost sight of the religious frame of reference which could have aided him. When the episode is over, the **protagonist** looks at his madonna figure, "wondering about something." But "even there," he says, "I could not put my finger on what I was wondering about."

CRITICISM

BÖLL AND THE CRITICS

In Germany, Böll has received the lion's share of critical attention among contemporary German writers. One reason is that he has written a great deal, another that he has been controversial. The central issue in the controversies seems to be the attempt by critics to do justice to a writer who seems to fall short of greatness in some of his work, but whose oeuvre nonetheless demands admiration, especially on human grounds. Böll is admired even by his severest critics.

Many of the most noteworthy views on Böll are contained in *In Sachen Böll; Ansichten und Aussichten* ed. Marcel Reich-Ranicki (Cologne, 1968). It includes assessments also by some non-German critics, but none by an American:

Cesare Cases (Italian) feels that Böll is no Kleist or Hebel, but "stylistically an often mediocre, at times even boring writer." But he praises Böll for his courage and admits that no living author has written a story as good as "Murke's Collected Silences."

Hermann Kesten (Germany) is one of Böll's strong defenders on artistic grounds. He is attracted by the style, to a "certain casualness in the movements of his prose, his humorous manner in which he unexpectedly improvises . . . and enunciates intense emotions in a fashion that make them sound like arguments."

Gustav Korlen (Swedish) describes the immense popularity of Böll in Sweden and gives a resume of critical voices from his country. "The scale runs from unqualified admiration to the insistent skepticism of a Stig Jonasson. But even this critic, whom I normally respect very highly, was finally converted by *The Clown*, of which he wrote: 'I was not able to detect the alleged greatness of Böll, therefore I am happy to be able to say now that Böll has almost caught up with his fame.'" Korlen sees Böll's style as "clear and clean . . . with which is connected the believability of the social criticism in Böll's work."

No less a critic than the Marxist George Lukacs admired Böll. He places him in the tradition of the great humanistic writers of the nineteenth century: "I hope Heinrich Böll will not be offended by an old man who, basing himself on such very antiquated considerations, is sympathetic to his work." In connection with Johanna Fahmel's shot in *Billiards at Half-Past Nine*, Lukacs says: "The 'senseless' shot of a crazy woman... is one of the few genuinely human attempts to come to terms with the fascist past in Germany."

The well-known German writer Siegfried Lenz admires the strength of suffering in Böll's characters: "They remain loyal to their suffering. Indeed, they defend themselves against their environment by confirming their suffering."

Hans-Egon Holthusen (German) defines Böll's strength differently. It lies not in the "creation of unforgettable characters, but in the capture and shaping of moods, views, perspectives, milieus, atmospheric conditions, which are characteristic for West German society. The sultry prosperity of this society and the moral depression of its sense of self, the superficial, hectic, blindly restorative element... [all this] in the melancholic-sarcastic language Böll found for these things; that is the genuine contribution of this author to the formation of the consciousness of a contemporary German." "Everyone," he sums up, "is agreed that Böll is overpoweringly likeable, only few people can escape this effect."

Joachim Kaiser (German) defends Böll's use of religious symbols and metaphors: "After repeated reading, years later, I suddenly feel I have understood that Böll is right after all: He did not want to place his truths into the **cliches** of rationalism, did not want to make them all too accessible."

Roy Pascal (English) singles out Böll as the writer who confronts the German past more tenaciously than any other.

Carl Amery (German) emphasizes that Böll must be seen ultimately as a conservative: "His anger indicts existing structures for endangering or even destroying simple values that further order. In this sense he naturally is also a revolutionary - a Catholic revolutionary... the German public has in Böll a great literary representative of a meaningful conservative position."

U.S. CRITICISM OF BÖLL

In the United States, Böll criticism is largely confined to reviews in newspapers and weekly journals, although there are some scholarly articles in literary journals (see Annotated Bibliography). Böll's reception in this country is, in a sense, analogous to that in Germany. Although with reservations, Böll has generally been taken as a morally serious and capable writer. Some of his books have been judged an unqualified success by individual reviewers, but none has been universally acclaimed. Up to *Group Portrait with Lady*, it was *The Clown* which received the most serious attention among Böll's works. When he received the Nobel Prize, it was called Böll's recognized masterpiece in the Jesuit journal *America*, notwithstanding the fact that this journal had earlier roundly rejected *The Clown*. Beginning with *The Clown*, Böll has been treated to a considerable degree as a religious writer. In contrast to the approbation of *The Clown* by some reviewers stands Anthony West's view that it is "an even shallower affair than his war novellas-a maudlin work." Patrick Crutwell echoes this rejection. To him, the novel moves "in an acrid, self-pitying way."

Though such extreme criticism of Böll's tendency to emotionality have been few, there has been persistent objection to his sentimentality. Thus J. Bauke, e.g., in the *New York Times Book Review*, questions Böll's belief that "goodness is where the heart is: left of center" as naive and somewhat smug. Böll having received the Nobel Prize, the advent in English of *Group Portrait with Lady* generated numerous reviews. By and large, they continue the pattern of mixed reactions. It was praised by *The National Observer* for the dense vital richness of its humanity and buried by *Time* as "stillborn" fiction. Melvin Maddox, in *Atlantic*, provides choices for the reader, who in *Group Portrait with Lady* can like Böll for "having heart," or dislike him for "being sentimental."

Newsweek feels that American readers can no longer afford to ignore Böll: "Böll is an acerb, intelligent, unglamorous writer who inspires only muted respect in this country . . . *Group Portrait with Lady* may change all that. It is no way thrilling or enchanting, but it has a dry, stubborn attraction. One finally comes to like a novelist who so resolutely declines to charm us."

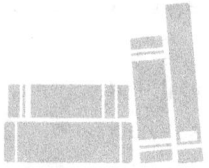

ESSAY QUESTIONS AND ANSWERS

Question: What Elements Constitute Böll Popularity in West and East?

Answer: To speak of Böll's popularity in West and East may seem to be too sweeping a statement to the American reading public. Böll is anything but a household word in this country. Confining ourselves to German writers, we could name several who have made a much greater impact on the American reader. There are the "classic" writers, Mann and Kafka; there is Brecht, and of course there is Hesse who without question is a household word among the young in this country. Among the contemporary writers, there is Grass who has even appeared on the cover of *Time* magazine. Even a suburban bookstore is likely to have his latest book. But Böll? to find out how well known he is, I went to a bookstore located in a huge suburban shopping center. There I found Grass' *Diary of a Snail*, but could not find a single person among the sales staff who had ever heard of Böll, notwithstanding that he was the year's Nobel Prize winner.

Popularity of foreign writers in America seems is some cases to be a matter of happenstance. When Hesse's American publisher complained to him that his books were not selling here, Hesse intimated in his reply not only that he was not surprised, but that he was proud of the lack of acceptance of his work in America, for to Hesse America stood for the very opposite of what he envisioned as a cultured society. Probably causing Hesse the discomfort that is said to cause people to turn around in their graves, his books subsequently became bestsellers, now available even in paperback gift sets. Böll is still obscure in America, and he is not likely to become a hot item on the America book market. Two factors speak against him. His ideas are not esoteric like Hesse's. Böll, one could argue, is a square. Second, he translates poorly. To draw on Hesse once more for comparison: Hesse translates very well. Those who think of Hesse as a poor stylist would maintain that, in fact, he improves in translation. Böll, on the other hand, at his best is a superb stylist, a superb literary craftsman and a writer with a truly admirable literary intelligence. This some Americans have already recognized, among them no less a figure than Joseph Heller; and more will recognize it, to be sure.

The surprise with which the American press reacted to the news that Böll had been awarded the Nobel Prize was not echoed in the rest of the Western world. One reason could be that Böll translates better into Swedish or French, for instance. Another is that Europeans bring a different outlook to Böll. The squareness, the moralistic stance Böll takes seem old-fashioned to Americans who only now are in the process of liberating themselves from the moral authority of the churches. The impact of the churches in much of Europe as a moral force on the conscience of the individual has been rather small for decades. Consequently, Böll does not seem so old-fashioned to the Europeans, but refreshingly committed. In much of Europe moral relativism is old hat; it is beginning to be a bore. Furthermore, Böll is not dogmatic; he by and large is not a preacher, but weaves his religious convictions so well into the fabric of his work that they enhance, rather than obscure its brightness. Böll, in other words, strikes the European reader as a believer, as a Christian humanist where all around the "Christians" seem to ride the coattails of religion for political and social reasons. Böll himself defines this attitude toward him when he has Hans Schnier say of himself that everyone likes him, even though he tells them all to go to hell.

It seems odd indeed that a Christian author is one of the most popular writers in the East. There are several explanations for this. Böll is a humanist with a special love for the people on the lower strata of society. Böll is always vigorously against the establishment, especially against the Catholic Church. This finds favor in the East. Furthermore, in several of his works, *Tomorrow and Yesterday*, and *Group Portrait with Lady*, to name but two, Russians are sympathetically drawn. The ordinary Socialist reader is probably impressed favorably by the fact that Böll grants his characters moral choices. He emphasizes the individual, and indicts the collective whenever it becomes oppressive to the individual. Furthermore, it is known that Russian readers, for example, feel that Böll is one of their own kind, not ideologically, but stylistically. The **epic** tempo and breadth in some of Böll's novels is reminiscent of Russian novels.

Böll's popularity increases wherever readers know about Böll's personality. He is the one West German writer one could imagine in the defiant role that Sakharov and Biermann play in their countries. The Socialist reader would like this trait especially. In the Socialist view the work of the artist must be a reflection of the values to which he subscribes as a person. To the Western reader this harmony of Böll's life and work is indeed a rare phenomenon. So often do we witness incompatibilities between the man and his work that we have to take refuge in the adage "Never trust the writer, trust his work." In the case of Böll, we can trust both.

Question: How Does Böll Treat His Female Figures?

Answer: Judging by *Tomorrow and Yesterday*, one would imagine Böll to have a preference for women as main figures. In this novel, the situation is definitely matriarchal. But this applies only to the family setting, not to public life. There the Gaselers and Schurbigels are in charge. They are the survivors of the war who, specifically in the case of Gaseler, are alive at the expense of others, such as Nella's husband. The male world is in charge in Germany. The protest of the women is ineffective. The hate the Bach family has for Gaseler cannot touch him.

In *Billiards at Half-Past Nine*, Johanna Fahmel, the most important female figure in the book, stages another ineffectual protest when she shoots at the minister of state. However, she does not seem as silly in the process as Nella and her mother who are ludicrous failures at fixing the roof of their house. Albert, on the other hand, manages to repair the roof in no time. There can be no doubt that Böll sketches a man's world in his works. But Böll never fails to recognize the inherent strength of women. In this sense Leni Pfeiffer, actually the only central woman-figure Böll has created, is not new. In addition to Johanna Fahmel, Nella and her mother, Hans Schnier's Marie is a woman of fortitude. She stays with Schnier for a number of years despite massive pressure by her friends to leave him. Schnier's mother is a primitive matriarchal figure, very strong as a survivor. The protagonist's wife in "Like a Bad Dream" is the tougher partner in her marriage, and the same is true, though in a very different sense, in "And there Was the Evening and the Morning." But there emerges no clear-cut pattern in addition to the basic strength of Böll's women. They may be totally immoral; they may have moral fortitude bordering on saintliness, but they can hardly be called central figures.

The question now is why does Böll in *Group Portrait with Lady* make a woman the central character? What is more, why does he make her a figure of nearly mythical dimensions? There is simply no male figure in Böll who has as much depth as Leni Pfeiffer in bridging contradictions and combining irreconcilable opposites.

No male in Böll's works emerges as such a powerful symbol of wholeness. The men in Böll, one is moved to conclude, are incapable of being true existential figures. They are bound to ideologies, like the Nettlingers, or they oppose an ideology, like Fahmel, or suffer from an ideology, like Hugo, but they are not really what they are without reference to a set of ideas even if it is only the notion of play, as is the case with Leni's father. Only Schnier is an exception. But whereas Leni has an inner calm, Hans Schnier at best can be the sneering social critic.

All this points to a full scale declaration of bankruptcy for Böll's world of men as ideologists. If the world of men, the patriarchal world, is in shambles, it is quite logical that Böll should come up with a woman as a figure of hope for the repair of the fragmentation men have wrought. Great writers have always recognized the restorative and even redemptive power of woman. We have only to think of Dante's Beatrice and Goethe's Gretchen. Leni Pfeiffer falls into the same category. She is Böll's statement of faith that the debilitating antitheses, call them mind and soul, instinct and intellect, emotion and reason, which men through the ages have declared to be unbridgeable and permanent, are in fact not at all forever beyond synthesis. Had Böll chosen a male figure to be like Leni, he would have indeed strained our credulity for the male as the shaper of our world has a record of villainy that reaches back into the millennia. He has disqualified himself as the existential saint with which Böll wishes to confront us in *Group Portrait with Lady*.

BIBLIOGRAPHY

WORKS BY HEINRICH BÖLL

Several of Böll's works are in the process of being retranslated, reprinted, and issued in paperback, reflecting a growing interest in Böll. In each instance below, the date refers to the original date of publication in English. The listing follows the order in which the works appeared in Germany:

The Train Was on Time, transl. by Richard Graves. London: Arco, 1956.

Traveller, If You Come to Spa. transl. by Mervyn Savill. London: Arco, 1956.

Adam, Where Art Thou, transl. by Mervyn Savill. New York: Criterion Books, 1955.

Acquainted with the Night, transl. by Richard Graves. New York: Holt, 1954.

Tomorrow and Yesterday, anonymous translation. New York: Criterion Books, 1957.

The Bread of Our Early Years, trans. by Mervyn Savill. London: Arco, 1957.

Irish Journal, transl. by Leila Vennewitz. New York: McGraw-Hill, 1967.

Billiards at Half-Past Nine, transl. by Patrick Bowles. London: Weidenfeld and Nicolson, 1961.

The Clown, transl. by Leila Vennewitz. New York: McGraw-Hill, 1965.

Absent Without Leave, transl. by Leila Vennewitz. New York: McGraw-Hill, 1965.

18 Stories, transl. by Leila Vennewitz. New York: McGraw-Hill, 1966.

The End of a Mission, transl. by Leila Vennewitz. New York: McGraw-Hill, 1968.

Group Portrait with Lady, transl. by Leila Vennewitz. New York: McGraw-Hill, 1973.

BOOKS AVAILABLE IN PAPERBACK

Billiards at Half-Past Nine, The Clown, 18 Stories.

CRITICAL LITERATURE ON BÖLL

German

Der Schriftsteller Heinrich Böll, Munchen: Deutscher Taschenbuch-Verlag, 1968. Includes a number of significant articles favorable to Böll. The contributors are mostly German. A bibliography of Böll's works. List of translations of Böll's works into other languages. A bibliography of studies on Böll. Indispensable to the serious student of Böll.

Schwarz, Wilhelm Johannes. *Der Erzahler Heinrich Böll*, Bern and Munchen: Francke Verlag, 1968. A critical study of

Böll's major works and figures. Its purpose is to show how Böll deals with the war and post-war problems. To Schwarz, Böll is unlikely to survive his early fame. But he concedes that some of his short stories will maintain their reputation as "classics." This study has been faulted by reviewers as being somewhat superficial.

In Sachen Böll, ed. by Marcel Reich-Ranicki. Koln: Kiepenheuer and Witsch, 1968. An anthology of significant articles and reviews on Böll by mostly German critics. A bibliography of Böll's works.

Jeziorkowski, Klaus. *Rhythmus und Figur*, Bad Homburg v.d.H.: Gehlen, 1968. An excellent study of Böll's literary craftsmanship, dealing mainly with *Billiards at Half-Past Nine* and "The Thrower-Away".

English

Bronson, David. "Böll's Women." *Monatshefte*, Vol. 57 (1965), pp. 291-300. An analysis of the male-female relationships in Böll's works. Women are a means of changing men's moral fiber. Böll's view of the ideal woman is basically traditional, yet he assigns to her alone the guardianship of moral standards and social conscience.

Conard, Robert C. "Two Novels About Outsiders: The Kinship of J.D. Salinger's *The Catcher in the Rye* with Heinrich Böll's *Ansichten eines Clowns*." *University of Dayton Review*, Vol. 5 (1968-1969), pp. 23-27. Conard sees a considerable influence of Salinger's book on Böll's *The Clown*. There are striking similarities between the heroes, major and minor characters, and the role of the film and the telephone. The central conflict in both novels depicts the moral person caught in a world of phonies. Both heroes reject the existing order and become its victims.

Klieneberger, H. R. "Heinrich Böll in *Ansichten eines Clowns.*" *German Life and Letters*, Vol. 19 (1965), pp. 34-39. Discussion of *The Clown* in relation to Böll's literary non-conformism. Böll refuses to be categorized as an esthetic writer, nor does he allow his characters and social criticism to be schematized. Klieneberger thinks highly of Böll as a social critic. *The Clown* cannot be dismissed as mere polemic.

Plant, Richard. "The World of Heinrich Böll." *German Quarterly*, Vol. 33 (1960), pp. 125-131. Interpretation of the world created by Böll as a waste land, where the heroes are victims and the mood is indifferent dispair.

Reid, J. H. "Time in the Works of Heinrich Böll." *Modern Language Review*, Vol. 62 (1967), pp. 476-486. Analysis of Böll's concern for the past. His experience of the years 1933-45, as a break with tradition, colors the content and form of his works. Böll's moral conscience condemns the escape from reality, while his artistic sensibility leans toward the abolition of time.

Waidson, Herbert Morgan. "The Novels and Stories of Heinrich Böll." *German Life and Letters*, Vol. 12 (1959), pp. 266-273. A descriptive chronological survey of Böll's works from 1949-1957. Some attention is devoted to style, form, and Böll's line of development. A very positive assessment of Böll.

Ziolkowski, Theodore. "Heinrich Böll. Conscience and Craft." *Books Abroad*, Vol. 34 (1960), pp. 213-222. Ziolkowski pinpoints Böll's credo as an artist and the basic elements of a typical Böll story. Compares him to Hemingway, Faulkner, Salinger, and Thomas Wolfe.

———. "Albert Camus and Heinrich Böll." *Modern Language Notes*, Vol. 77 (1962), pp. 282-291. Although Böll is a devout Catholic and Camus an atheist, both are seen here basically as moralists and severe critics of their societies. Both recognize the modern conflict between reality and idealism, and they both sympathize with the lowly and victimized.

———. "The Inner Veracity of Form." *Books Abroad*, Vol. 47, (1972), pp. 17-24. Occasioned by Böll's winning of the Nobel Prize, Ziolkowski analyzes Böll's stature in terms of his work and his role as a chronicler of Germany during the midcentury. In this role he sees Böll as the successor to Mann and Hesse.

www.ingramcontent.com/pod-product-compliance
Lightning Source LLC
LaVergne TN
LVHW011723060526
838200LV00051B/3007